THE TRUTH LIES WITH GETHSEMANE HOUSE

By Clare Curtis

FOR ZOË

Incident Report Form
Venue: Gethsemane House, Bishops Road, London
Time Incident Reported: 8:00 AM
Police Incident Number: 2008666
Case Officer: DCI John Polglase
Witnesses (Names and Contact Numbers):
Thomas Carrigan - 07995783787
Brief Description of Report:

A neighbour reported a possible case of false imprisonment and raised concerns about unethical scientific experiments being conducted at a nearby property. Participation appears to be non-consensual, with the neighbour (a doctor/surgeon) having been asked to assist. He reported that the experiments were unlike anything he had encountered in his medical career. He believes the testing is radical and potentially illegal, suggesting it is being conducted without proper clinical oversight. He indicated the need for urgent intervention and medical assistance. The experiments are located in a separate annexe behind the kitchen, accessible via a steel door with a keypad.

1

September 12th, 2013

I had been thoroughly briefed. It would start with a small chip being injected into the visual cortex at the back of my brain. I would be placed under general anaesthesia, and my mind would do the rest. I could taste, smell, touch, feel, and see everything as vividly as if it were a normal day. The fine print was chilling: I would believe everything that happened. If I jumped off a building, my brain could, even for a moment, convince me that I was dead.

Madeleine, in a rare moment of affection, tried to reassure me. "Nothing bad will happen, you're too important to risk."

"What if I get hit by a car?" I asked.

"Then you'd go to the hospital like anyone else, Elizabeth. I know you tend to panic, but try not to. Just do the mundane things you normally do. No juggling knives or leaping between buildings," she said with a small smile. "We've run thousands of scenarios with participants. Remember, you're lying in a lab with three medically trained scientists overseeing every thought and movement."

As Delilah prepared the aesthetic, Madeleine added, "There's one minor side effect I didn't mention, because you'd overreact." Just hearing the word "overreact" made my heart race.

"There's a minuscule chance your subconscious could believe the simulation is real," she muttered casually. Seeing the look of abject horror on my face, she elaborated. "This happened once, with a participant who was schizophrenic, someone who hadn't informed us of their condition. You're not schizophrenic, right?"

"Which one of us are you talking to?" I snapped, trying to steady my voice.

"Lib, I promise you; I wouldn't put you through this if A) you hadn't begged me to, and B) I thought there was even the slightest risk. It's six hours. You'll have the best week! And if we notice anything, so much as an elevated heartbeat, I'll pull you out. Trust me."
"You told me never to trust anyone who says, 'trust me.'"
"And I was right!" she laughed. "Just relax. We'll give you a little 'happy injection,' and then once you're settled, we'll administer the anaesthetic."
"'Happy injection'?"
"Midazolam. You'll wake up in the simulation feeling sleepy, so listen to your body; you still need rest."
Jude placed an oxygen mask over my face. A wave of claustrophobia hit me, and his cold, penetrating eyes made me uneasy. As I struggled for air, his unsettling gaze stayed fixed on me until everything went black.

September 15th, 2008

No one I knew was attending the same university. My family had decided from the moment I was born that I would be the one to go to Oxford. Instead of a rattle, they placed a flute in my hands. Neither of my parents could play an instrument, so naturally, I should. They were living vicariously through me, having never quite made it themselves.

My mum, the local GP, had seen (as she put it) "everyone's genitals", though she quickly clarified, "in a professional capacity." My father worked in IT, a job he openly despised, which sparked countless lectures that began with, "You need to go to a good university, so you don't end up like me," as he washed down his seventh beer.

When my acceptance letter arrived, my mum screamed so loudly that I worried the neighbours might call the police. The same neighbours she always invited over so I could play piano for them. "Isn't she incredible? She'll play the Royal Albert Hall one day." (I did.) For someone who was an introvert, it was deeply embarrassing.

Receiving a music scholarship pleased my father. The money they'd saved could now be spent on something "fun," though he wasn't sure how to have fun anymore. Eventually, he decided "fun" was Carole from accounting.

Leaving home for the first time, I was thrilled. The constant refrain of "while you're under our roof, you'll follow our rules" would no longer apply. I would be free. I wasn't even sure what I wanted, but I knew I wanted it. I took a gap year to travel, a decision both parents opposed.
They were still together when they drove me through Oxford's ornate gates, my mum leaning out of the window like an excited dog with Grandad's old Nikon. As we hauled my belongings from the car, Mum spoke to every person in sight. "She seemed nice." "Lizzy, that boy had a clarinet—you should talk to him." I ushered them back to the car, then watched to make sure they drove away. Moments later, my phone buzzed: "Make us proud."

The first few weeks were hard. Everyone was perfectly pleasant, but they weren't my people. They seemed to want only to study; no one was interested in having fun. One night, after a tame game of Bridge in Christina's room (eight beers shared among ten people), I called Lisa to see if she was struggling too. I could barely hear her over the screaming and cheering. "It's my turn, I'll call you tomorrow!" she shouted and hung up. She didn't.

I sat back in my tiny dorm room and watched *Sex and the City* for the seventh time. I sobbed as I drifted off to sleep. The moment I'd waited so long for, which I'd imagined as the most incredible time of my life, was turning out to be the loneliest. I missed my friends. I even missed my horrendous family.

That Friday, I went to the Sheldonian Theatre to meet the orchestra. It was stunning. The ceiling was adorned with thirty-two removable oil paintings by Robert Streater and seeing it in person took my breath away. Around thirty people sat eagerly clutching their instruments (a phrase I'd later use in an article that no one else found funny).

One girl lay across three chairs, staring at the ceiling. Her long blonde hair spilled over the edge of the chair, and large Audrey Hepburn sunglasses shielded her eyes. One by one, members introduced themselves, listing their musical accolades. Suddenly, the girl let out an audible sigh. Robert Portman, the conductor, put down his pen and called out, "I see Madeleine Magdalene has graced us with her presence! Do you mind, Madeleine?"

"Not at all, Bob," she groaned back, her accent unmistakably Australian.

"In fact, Madeleine, why don't you be the first to come up and perform for our new recruits?"
Madeleine rose slowly, like Bela Lugosi rising from his coffin. She made her way to the stage with an air of indifference, wearing a mini dress, Converse sneakers, and an oversized men's suit jacket. She reached for a violin as Robert smirked. He knew, despite her cavalier attitude, her lateness, her drunkenness, that she was an exquisite musician. She serenaded the room with *Nocturne No. 20 in C-sharp Minor*. It was flawless. The room remained silent until the end when a roar of applause echoed through the theatre. Madeleine sloped back to her makeshift lounger as if nothing had happened. One by one, everyone else took to the stage, all aware that they couldn't top her performance.

I wasn't thrilled when my turn came. I loved performing, but only when hidden among other musicians. Solo recitals filled me with anxiety. I played an allegro excerpt from Franz Liszt's *Liebestraum*. Everyone loves Franz Liszt.

From the stage, I noticed Madeleine had sat up. She took off her sunglasses and leaned forward, elbows on her knees. When I finished, she gave me a standing ovation, whistling and clapping wildly. "That's how you play a fucking piano!" she bellowed.

As I stepped down, she gestured to an empty chair beside her. I pretended not to see. So, she came to me.
"That was exquisite. You were exquisite!"
"Thanks," I replied, turning to face the stage.
"Truly, you're a virtuoso. Someone needs to get that piano a cigarette after that performance."
I kept looking forward.
"This is worse than my grandmother's funeral. And I loved that woman. We need to leave." I hoped ignoring her would work, but she stood up.
"We're leaving." It wasn't a request. She took my arm and dragged me out before I could respond. She was surprisingly strong for someone so tiny.

2

Madeleine Magdalene

Madeleine's familiarity with Robert stemmed from the fact that this was her fifth year at Oxford, despite being only twenty-one. She was a bona fide genius. Her brain was a sponge, and Oxford was an ocean of information. Her family, originally from Sydney, had moved to England when she was fourteen. Her father was also an extraordinarily talented scientist, and her mother, originally from Pretoria, met him in Cape Town while visiting her brother. Madeleine's uncle adored her and decided to help fund her education after her IQ was determined to be 180. He bought the family a stately home overlooking Hampstead Heath, and when her parents moved back to Australia when Madeleine was twenty, she stayed.

She was a self-confessed recluse and was obsessed with research. She would disappear for weeks, sometimes months, at a time. Like a dog with a bone, she couldn't let go of an idea until she got to the bottom of it. Her attention to detail was exceptional, though the intensity of her focus could be unsettling. She loved math because there was no ambiguity, and science because there was so much.

We ended up sitting outside a bar in the midday sun. Madeleine ordered two Bloody Marys. one for medicinal purposes and one for sipping. When they arrived, she used the celery to hold back the ice and downed the first in one go. "Don't judge me," she muttered. We instantly felt comfortable around each other. I felt drawn in to her orbit. She was animated by even the smallest coincidence. Her mother was also named Elizabeth. She rarely spoke of her family during the years I knew her. Her mother disappeared one day, and her father, overwhelmed by grief, changed. He spiralled into what Madeleine called a "rabbit hole of despair." If Madeleine didn't want to talk about something, she simply wouldn't. If pressed, she would leave.

"Tell me, Elizabeth," she began, "how much do you despise everyone here?"
The question took me by surprise. I mumbled something about everyone seeming nice.
"Do you really mean that? Because your eyelids are puffy, your eyes look glassy, and I don't sense you're hungover. I don't see smile lines, and you look riddled with sadness."
It was a relief to finally release my feelings. Madeleine leaned back and sipped her drink, nodding as I spoke.

"I've tried so hard! Especially for someone who finds it difficult to fit in. But everyone is just so," I searched for the right word.
"Fucking dull."
"Yes! Dull! I tried to find common ground, to see the best in people. Do you know how many cans of beer I saw go out to the recycling after a week in a dorm of ten students? Twenty. There were eight empty wine bottles, all mine. It feels like a retirement home."

"Doesn't it feel good to get that off your chest? I lasted two weeks before deciding to commute."
Her, the motivated, studious careerist. Me, the undriven, insecure introvert. Her, fearless and outspoken. Me, conflict-averse and discreet. We seemed to be opposites, yet we were drawn to each other.
Madeleine had a way of getting people to do whatever she wanted and making them feel privileged for it. She had charisma that shone even in the darkest rooms. Despite her small stature, she had a commanding presence, as though she wielded some unseen power. She peered through the window to get the bartender's attention; he was already watching her. She motioned for another round, and he appeared at our table within minutes.

Madeleine looked me up and down before announcing, "You look like Winona Ryder."

I took a sip of my wine. "In the Johnny Depp days or the shoplifting days?"
"Oh, the Johnny Depp days. You've got a classic look, the dark hair, the gorgeous brown eyes. We just need to get them sparkling again."

We spoke for hours, drinking at a pace even I wasn't used to. Madeleine glanced at her watch and asked what I was doing for the weekend. I had nothing planned. "That long silence means nothing." She stood, drained her almost-full glass, and motioned for me to do the same. "We're going to my place."

I overthought everything. Who was this girl? What if she lived in a slum? What if her friends were like her, but in a bad way? What if I ended up stuck in London and got mugged and sold to traffickers? The usual worries. But I shrugged and said, "Sure, why not." It was out of character, but the alternative was another night sobbing into a cheap bottle of wine. Madeleine pulled out a wad of cash and left it under the empties. I looked at her, perplexed. "That's almost £100."
"It's fine," she said, baffled by my reaction. "I have more." And she did.

Madeleine skipped over to a black Mercedes parked outside. It was impeccably clean, the kind of car dignitaries used. She opened the back door and curtsied, gesturing for me to get in. I must have looked terrified because Madeleine tried to reassure me. "You don't have to panic. I know him." I stood frozen.
"Elizabeth, this isn't an abduction. Get in the car."

"Miss Madeleine," grumbled the driver as Madeleine hugged him from behind, her arms wrapped around the headrest. "This is Jude. I'm his surrogate daughter. Jude, this is Libby."
"A pleasure, Libby, I'm sure. Home, Ms. Madeleine? Or shall we save time and go straight to the hospital for a stomach pump?"

"Isn't he the funniest?" Madeleine laughed, popping a bottle of champagne from nowhere, startling us all.

Jude raised his eyebrows and drove on, grimacing into the rearview mirror as Madeleine offered him a glass. Madeleine talked nonsense for the entire drive, pausing only when a song she liked came on the radio, at which point she would leap into the front to turn up the volume. Jude seemed used to her antics; through his grumbling and eye-rolling, I caught the occasional smirk. She was a nightmare, but like a reckless puppy, she was impossible to stay mad at.
We drove through a quaint hamlet with traditional shops and ornate storefronts, adorned with floral hanging baskets and old-fashioned bicycles. It didn't feel like London, not the London I imagined. We turned onto a country lane, and the houses grew more luxurious the further we went. I looked to my left and gasped at the sight of Hampstead Heath framed by the London skyline. It was breathtaking.

The road ended in a turning circle, where two large wrought-iron gates began to open, revealing manicured hedges lining a driveway. At the end of the drive stood a grand mansion, a stately home fit for royalty, with Georgian sash windows, lion statues flanking the stairs, and a polished gold knocker on the door. I chuckled to myself. Of course, the enigmatic girl with £400 sunglasses and a private chauffeur lived here.

Madeleine didn’t look for my reaction. She sipped her champagne as though it were juice. I wanted to ask if she was some kind of heiress, but I didn't want to pry. I defaulted to silence, which never served me well.

Madeleine opened her door and asked if I was coming. "Jude isn’t my chauffeur, Elizabeth," she teased. I turned beetroot red.

Jude got out and squeezed her shoulder. "It is absolutely not a pleasure... ever," he said, leaning in to kiss her cheek. He looked at me and forced a smile, though I could tell he didn't trust me. I felt a peculiar unease.

Madeleine was devoted to Jude, later explaining that he was always protective and suspicious of her new friends. He couldn't let anything to happen to her. The mystery of her father remained. No matter how close I got to Jude, or how much I tried to probe, just the mention of her father would rile him. He made it abundantly clear: "We do not talk about that man, especially around Madeleine."

"Who is he?" I asked Madeleine as he drove off.
"My father's ex-business partner. Welcome to Gethsemane House!" she announced, her voice mocking a strong English accent.

Madeleine swung open the front door, revealing a double-height ceiling adorned with the most decadent furnishings. She flung the gentleman's jacket she'd been carrying onto a yellow ochre velvet chaise longue, and clapped her hands, prompting the gentle whirling of Debussy to flow through the hall. When I asked if I could look around, she replied, "Knock yourself out. I'm making Bellinis."

Each room was meticulously decorated with furniture that complemented the age of the building. Everything was undeniably beautiful and spotless; however, it felt staged and unused, something Madeleine later confirmed, saying she only used four of the twenty-four rooms and four bathrooms. Nobody needed three entrance rooms.

Each room was as large as the home I grew up in, most of them resembling museum displays. The library, which also doubled as a music room, was a sanctuary for the arts. It had previously served as a ballroom, and original photographs of galas held here were hung in gilded frames on the panelled walls. A bookshelf ran from floor to ceiling along one wall, filled with literature, first editions bound in leather, encyclopaedias, and science books. A large fireplace stood before two perfectly placed red leather Chesterfield sofas, brought together with a coffee table and a chess set carved from Peruvian marble.

A pristine gramophone (which still worked) stood proudly next to a designated bar area, where crystal decanters and glassware rested on a green art deco table. Large sets of French double doors ran across one wall, framing the magnificent view and flooding the room with light. A harpsichord, a Steinway grand piano, and a cello stood proudly before some rose-pink velvet club chairs, beneath which a four-metre Persian rug lay on dark herringbone wood floors. Then I saw it, mounted on the wall in a glass case: an original Stradivarius. It was probably worth more than the house itself. Surely it couldn't be real. Except it was.

I wandered towards the kitchen, passing room after room of opulence. There were lighter patches of maroon along the hallway where photos had clearly once hung. For such a large family home, filled with photos and portraits of every other generation, there wasn't a single photo of Madeleine's family.

The kitchen was surprisingly modern in contrast to the rest of the house. A large American-style fridge dominated the sleek and polished chef's dream of a space. It led through to a formal dining room with a large table set for sixteen, which again looked like it had last been used during the First World War. A less formal orangery led off from the kitchen to the sculpted gardens. More fountains, more statues, exotic trees, and shrubs (some I'd never seen before), a rare fish enclosure, and yet another stunning view. "If you like this view, you should see it from upstairs," she called out as she handed me a peach-coloured drink.

She was right; the balcony view from Madeleine's room was even better. We ended up spending virtually every evening there. As the sun disappeared behind the city's silhouette, we would lie on the sun loungers beneath blankets, sipping whatever improvised alcoholic concoction Madeleine had devised that afternoon. Her bedroom, though, was incredibly bare for someone so charismatic. The furnishings lacked any sign of her personality.

The only items were a large four-poster bed, an Eames chair in the corner with a few garments strewn across it, and a bedside table with a stack of books and an old-fashioned banker's desk lamp. The walls were painted in a slightly bluish-white, Farrow & Ball style, with large, gilded frames containing copies of 'The Scream,' 'Soir Bleu,' and 'Morning Sun', which, for all I knew, could have been originals.

As we continued the tour, each room we entered revealed more sparse furnishing, just like Madeleine's, with no sign of other occupants. At this stage, I'd had quite a few drinks, and as we walked down the grand staircase towards the library, I asked, "Is it just you living here?" She nodded and replied, "Uh-huh." "So, I mean... where are your parents?" She looked me dead in the eyes and, without much emotion, said, "They left." Before I could ask more, we walked into the library, and she turned on all the chandeliers one by one. "Quick, let's play some music, and then we can get some wine and watch the sun go down. Shall we start with some Chopin?"
Though we had only just met, my curiosity outweighed caution. The situation was bizarre enough as it was. I decided not to pry further. Madeleine was open about everything else, so this must have been a subject she wasn't comfortable discussing with a stranger. Especially one she had kindly invited into her home, plied with fine cocktails, and entertained with exquisite violin performances. It was the first time in a long while that I didn't feel lonely. It felt as if I had known her my whole life. Our values and passion for music aligned, and her humour was sharp and constant. She had all the confidence, sass, and spontaneity I lacked, yet somehow, whenever I was around her, I felt less afraid of everything.

Out of nowhere, as if she'd spotted an armed intruder, she suddenly stopped playing the violin and screeched, "Oh my God!" For reasons I still don't understand, I screamed too. "Are you okay?" she asked, bewildered. "I just... I just thought..." But she was far too distracted to care. She grabbed my hand and almost pulled my arm from its socket as we dashed down the hallway. We raced through the kitchen, under a glass walkway that passed through an Italian-style courtyard, and into another building.

At the end, presumably the old servants' quarters, were two doors. "This is the lab." She punched in a key code and swung open the door to reveal a gigantic room filled with sophisticated equipment and computers. She started towards a spiral staircase that led to the roof. "This will blow your mind." Outside was an eight-metre telescope on the adjacent flat roof. "It's the second-largest telescope in the world. I discovered a comet when I was sixteen, and they let me name it."

"They?"

"NASA."

"Shut up! What did you name it? Can you name it anything you want?"

"Within reason. It appears in official reports, so you can't call it 'cometschlong.' It's usually named after the discoverer, so we called it 'Madrock.'"

"But this isn't even the exciting part."

We hurried back down the stairs, her enthusiasm fuelling my own. We left the lab and entered the second door, which had no theatrical entry system. It was a recording studio. A full studio, with enough instruments to equip an entire orchestra: another grand piano, Fender Stratocasters, Lowden acoustic guitars, drum sets, electric keyboards, fully soundproofed walls. "It has some of the best recording equipment in London. Winehouse recorded 'Back to Black' here."

"No fucking way."

"We always have tons of people asking for sessions here, mainly because nobody knows about it. This building holds so many secrets. The orchestra and I have been asked to play on a heap of albums. You'd be surprised how many artists don't realise how effective some strings and woodwinds are to a song."

It was insane. This entire house and its contents were the makings of a dream world. All that was missing was a swimming pool. (In 2012, during an unexpected heatwave, I made a flippant comment to this effect. By the end of the day, a trench was dug, and two weeks later, we had a heated infinity pool.)

Later, the moon shone brightly down on us as we let the soft piano music of Einaudi's 'La Scala' flow out onto the balcony.
"Tell me one thing no one knows," beamed Madeleine as she pulled a blanket over her legs.
Without even realising it, I blurted out, "I want to write a book." I surprised myself; I had never even thought about it before. I didn't even know I wanted to author a book. "What about you?" I asked, passing back the nearly finished joint that Madeleine had conveniently found in her dressing gown.
"I know I shouldn't… because most astrophysicists agree it isn't possible, and this never leaves the balcony of trust, but I still believe in the possibility of alien life."
Just after she said this, as I exhaled a cloud of smoke, a shooting star drifted slowly overhead, and we both squealed simultaneously, "Make a wish!"
In my head, I wished that I would meet a fun, handsome, romantic man, someone both smart and laid-back, someone I could curl up with to watch movies and eat pizza on a Friday night. I wanted to fall in love.

Aloud, Madeleine whispered, "I don't want to be alone anymore."
For no reason, after she'd said it, and I saw the sadness in her eyes and her the sympathy in mine, we laughed. We laughed until we couldn't remember what we were laughing about anymore.

I woke up the next day after the best night's sleep I'd had in months. The sound of Madeleine's alarm song, 'Wake Me Up Before You Go-Go,' seemed to penetrate the entire house. The French doors let in a gentle breeze as I snuggled under Egyptian cotton bedding. I could smell pastries and fresh coffee, so I threw on the guest dressing gown, the nicest robe I'd ever worn in my life. Madeleine was dancing around the kitchen to Fleetwood Mac, juicing oranges in time with the drumbeats.

"I've had an incredible idea!" She was full of beans. "We should throw a party here, tomorrow night! A proper party, with music and canapés and wild birds." It was 9 a.m. It was a lot to digest. "Help yourself to breakfast! I'll make a list!" She started to walk out, perhaps to a vintage bureau where she kept some quills and ink, when she turned back with uncertainty and asked, "That is, if you want to have a party? If not, I can drive you back to Oxford. I have a car."
"No! No, a party sounds fun. The wilder and more endangered the birds, the better."
Her face refilled with joy and deviousness as she scurried out of the room like a mischievous little mouse.

An hour or so later, after I'd showered and dressed, I made my way downstairs and followed the sound of Madeleine's laughter. She looked so elegant, sitting outside in the sunshine at the white cast-iron bistro set, wearing a long silk dressing gown with her phone to her ear and the other hand holding an espresso. Her laptop was open, displaying an organised folder of schemes, plans, invitations, and entertainment. One thing you could never fault Madeleine for was her organisational skills. She slapped shut her flip phone and looked at me with possessed eyes. "It's going to be fucking excellent!"

She patted the seat next to her and started running through guests. She asked if there was anyone I wanted to invite. Most of my friends were still finding their feet at university, and no one was particularly close by. Regardless, I sent a few messages out, which were declined as expected.

"SO… party plans so far. We have a fireworks display; we have the orchestra. old and new, we have canapés, we have a champagne fountain, we have someone coming to install lights in an hour, we have burlesque dancers, there's a guy on stilts to hand out drinks (though I'm not sure how that works), we have fire-breathers, we have a magician, we have…" she scrolled down her list and took a swig of orange juice, "a man on a unicycle who can also juggle. He says at a stretch he can hand out nibbles but refuses to be held liable if we serve gazpacho. We have a cocktail station, a fire-eater, a confetti cannon, a snow machine, low-lying fog, and doves. Do you think I've forgotten anything?"
"Dancing elephants?" I joked.
"Too short notice," she said, without a hint of sarcasm.
"You did all this? In just over an hour?"
Madeleine could see the astonishment in my eyes, and it pleased her greatly.

"So, the neighbours. Rory and Thomas are coming, they own next door. They're both surgeons, incredibly fun, very handsome, in their thirties. They're quite particular about not being stereotyped with all the gay clichés, but that said, they never say no to a party, so they're shooting themselves in the foot."

Madeleine then opened another file showing a street view image of the entire cul-de-sac, with each property included.

"The other next door, I'm almost 98.6% certain, is a government safe house. It's virtually always vacant, and when it isn't, secret-service-style bodyguards circle the perimeter with guns, and you never see the occupants—different cars each time. It's currently unoccupied."
"Next, next door, Mr and Mrs Petersson—really nice couple, a thousand years old—we'll invite them anyway."
"Next, next, next door right—Petra Zimmer. I used to see her walking her dog, but it's been a couple of years now—I don't think she's mobile anymore."

"Next, next door left, the Engelsteins. They're in Miami. They're always somewhere glamorous."
"Then this side, we have the Chans, who we love. They're coming. David at the end is probably away filming, but we'll knock anyway."

"This house"—she tentatively touched the photo with hesitation— "we never approach. These are the Boo Radleys of the neighbourhood. The malevolent phantoms. Abigail Veruschka and her daughter. She's some sort of practising gypsy, and she sends chills down my bones. Her house is the only one on the road that looks like it belongs in a Stephen King novel. We avoid it at all costs."
She continued listing the neighbours we would invite until it suddenly dawned on me.
"What are we going to wear?"

I realised I was still wearing yesterday's clothes and underwear. There was no way I was fitting into Madeleine's clothes; she was at least two dress sizes smaller than me. Madeleine put on a posh British accent and declared, "We must go to the shops!" before standing up and twirling around like a peacock in her Art Nouveau silk gown.
It's worth noting that at this point, when Madeleine read out her wild list of party entertainment, I, still unsure about her sense of humour, assumed she was half-joking. Like when someone says they've packed everything, including the kitchen sink.

We went out to the garage at the front left of the house, and she opened the triple doors to reveal some classic cars. I wasn't sure what they all were, but I recognised the eighties-style Porsche 911 that she started walking towards. She lowered the roof, wrapped a scarf around the loose bun on her head, slid on her sunglasses, applied red lipstick in the mirror, and as she drove out, hollered, "HOP IN, LADY!" We zoomed around the country lanes, the wind causing a tornado of parking tickets and fuel receipts inside the cabin. It wasn't long before we were stuck in slow-moving traffic, where it might have been quicker to walk. Smug cyclists revelled as they passed us, with their sensible mode of transport absolving them of their failure to fulfil their dreams.

We rolled up to Harrods, and Madeleine stepped out of the car, tossing her keys to the smartly dressed man at the door. "Good catch, Leonard! Park her up real nice."
"Of course, Ms Magdalene. Message me when you're ready to leave."

This was bananas. Who was this girl?! I was starting to get nervous. My budget was about £35 a day, so this was a bit out of my comfort zone. I'd let Madeleine pick her dress, then I'd pop down to Oxford Street and find something a bit more student friendly.

Every price tag I turned over made my eyeballs pop. Madeleine leaned in and whispered, "Darling, if you have to look at the price tag, you can't afford it."
"Madeleine, I can't afford it! I'll help you pick yours, then I'll venture down the street to grab something less like a mortgage payment."
"Absolutely not! This was my harebrained scheme. You let me buy you a dress. It's not even an argument. I want to get you a gift!"
"But the thing is, I need some underwear too, and I don't have any other clothes here or toiletries and—"

"Liberace, we'll stretch for some undies. I don't want to sound like an arsehole, but I'm rich and I don't care. It would upset me more if you said no."
Reluctantly, I agreed. I would find something in the sale and pay her back. I kept veering off towards the cheaper sections, only to be pulled back.
"We want something that says, Lady of the Manor, 1920s glamour chic."
"Got it!" yelped the sales assistant, who returned with the most incredible embellished floor-length dresses. After we tried some on and picked the ones we liked (neither of which had prices on), the deal was done. I asked how much they were, and to this day, I still don't know.

There was one more stop for shoes, a quick £15 cocktail, and then the car was waiting for us outside, shinier than when we'd left it. Throughout the shopping spree, Madeleine's phone kept buzzing, her alert tone a screaming cat.
"Everyone I invited is coming! Even Robert, and he's bringing the alumni orchestra!"
We arrived back at the house to find a white box tied with a black ribbon resting against the door. Madeleine untied the bow, pulled back the red tissue paper, and revealed gold-embossed invitations.

"How on earth did you get these designed, printed, and delivered so quickly?!" I asked, perplexed.
"Money," replied Madeleine. "Friends of my parents are designers. Their son is nifty with graphics and this kind of bedazzle!"
"Come, let's go for a walk. You can meet everyone on our road. Hand-delivered invites—such decadence!"
The gate next door buzzed open almost immediately as we approached the driveway, and Thomas called out over the intercom, "Come on in, darling."
"Remember," said Madeleine, "if you aren't sure what to say, humour is the answer."

Their house wasn't as dramatic as Madeleine's, but it was still nicer than any house I'd seen before hers. The garden was pristine, with a large, gravelled drive at the front of the house and two Mini Coopers parked side by side. The large door opened, and two Welsh terriers, George and Michael, came bounding towards us, almost crying with joy. Madeleine, who up until now had not shown much emotion about her absent family—which had concerned me a little—immediately fell to the ground in anticipation of the dogs. One hand per dog, she tussled, fussed, and petted them both, rubbing their bellies and scratching behind their ears. She pulled two dog treats from her sleeves like a magician, as I made small talk with Thomas. He was tall, athletic, and blonde, with kind eyes and a very striking maroon smoking jacket. A few minutes passed, and Madeleine was still just rollicking on the floor with the hounds.

"We'll both be there tomorrow. Rory is performing heart surgery until about five, so fingers crossed there are no complications."

"Oh well, I can't imagine things will get started until 7 pm," said Madeleine, tussling Michael's ears.

Nervously, I quipped, "I hope she's not talking about the patient undergoing heart surgery."

He stared, I stared, Madeleine stared—then suddenly, raucous laughter. "Good one," he said as he straightened his paisley cravat.

He called off the dogs as Madeleine got to her feet, brushing off the fur and detritus. "We'll see you both tomorrow!" she called out, not having been involved in the conversation. "If Rory doesn't lose heart," I added.

"Oh, Madeleine, I like your new friend. Such fun."

The next few neighbours were no-shows to the doorbell, so invites were posted. As we walked towards the next house, Madeleine turned to me and started walking backwards. "What can you smell?" she asked, again and again, as I started sniffing. I couldn't really smell anything. I took a guess with jasmine, which was denied. "Keep going." Then, as we passed the side of the garden, the wind changed, and suddenly there was a pungent waft of weed. We locked eyes. Madeleine explained that she'd been out walking one morning and noticed the unmistakable scent. She'd knocked on the door under the guise of looking for a lost cat. Dan Chan opened the door with eyes redder than a London bus. Dan lived with his wife Judy, his childhood sweetheart. Judy was a powerhouse and worked for one of the big banks, and Dan Chan, Ganja Man, was a music producer. Madeleine had hoped for some sort of grow-house situation, but sadly it was just Dan in the garden getting some inspiration.

"I guess they're in their thirties. Dan is an insane keyboard player, and you'd think he'd be the most fun because Judy must be so professional—but you'd be wrong. That woman is an animal. We had a party once, and there was a karaoke machine. I asked Judy if she was going to sing, and she snapped, 'Why, because I'm Asian?' Then she took a hit of ecstasy, slapped me around the face, and ran away. An hour later, I found her playing Flute Sonata by Sergei Prokofiev in the fountain. Absolutely blindsided. She was still wearing a two-piece suit and kitten heels. Apparently, she'd never played the flute before in her life."
The Chans opened the door, and it was impossible to gauge if they were pleased to see Madeleine or not. She handed them the invite, and it was the fastest "yes" I'd seen.
"Is Reg coming?"
"Yup."
As the door closed, I enquired, "Reg?"
"Yeah, Reg. Elton John."
I burst out laughing. Madeleine just looked at me and said, "OK then."

As we continued to walk down the row of immaculate properties, one stood out as completely different from the others. Run-down with a grey façade, it completely juxtaposed the freshly painted white mansions surrounding it. The rest of the street was full of colour, but this house was in black and white. It reminded me of the type of house that appears in every horror film—the one the kids dare each other to go to on Halloween. Its large stoop was surrounded by rusted Gothic-style ironwork, with Victorian iron wall brackets holding flower baskets filled with dead black weeds. Two gargoyles frowned down from the top of the turret-style tower, comprised of cracked, rotten wooden panels. It housed a series of splintered windows—the eyes of the house—which seemed to follow you as you moved. The air felt thicker as we approached the outer gates, barely hanging on their hinges, and a sudden feeling of hopelessness enveloped me.

I pushed aside the overgrown ivy that covered the house sign, revealing 'Veritas' carved ornately. Suddenly, I felt an overwhelming sense of being watched as my eyes caught something moving in the top floor window. An old, musty net curtain was fanning from a disturbance. Either the old house was playing tricks on me, or someone was spying on us. Madeleine noticed I had stopped and came back to fetch me.

"There it is the property that devalues the whole road. Never speak to that woman; she'll place a gypsy curse on you."
"What woman?"
As I turned around, with what must have been the speed of a springbok, Abigail Veruschka was standing at the gate. A slim Bulgarian lady in her early fifties with smooth long black hair, wearing clothes that didn't match her property. A tailored pair of trousers, a crisp white shirt pinned together at the collar by a cameo brooch, finished with a knee-length green velvet jacket. Her jewellery was gold and emerald, and by her well-applied make-up, she seemed more in keeping with the other residents than her house suggested.

"This woman. Lilith here."

Madeleine grabbed my arm, trying to drag me away as I felt transfixed by this woman. She had me in a trance. Her dazzlingly green eyes were almost hypnotic. It felt as though they were looking into my soul. I was distracted from her gaze by movement from the top window—this time, I glimpsed what appeared to be a teenage girl hiding in the attic room. She scurried as though she didn't want me to see her. She looked gaunt and distressed.

"Your house is purgatory," she began saying to Madeleine, and the further we walked away, the louder she spoke. "We all know what goes on in that house, and it isn't Christian." We started to pick up the pace, and then she shouted out, "You need to open your eyes!"

When Madeleine had described her and the house, I'd assumed she was exaggerating for dramatic effect, but I was genuinely terrified. I wanted to turn around to see if she was still standing there, but I was worried if I met her eyes again, I'd turn to stone. We were almost jogging to the next house, and as we reached the gate, I turned to Madeleine and gasped, "What the fuck was that all about?!"
"Lilith is mental. I don't think anything frightens me as much as that woman, and I've worked with plutonium. Everything about her—the way she looks so calm, the freaky house, the shit that leaves her evangelist mouth. Don't let her poison you with her mendacities. If she came to a Halloween party, I worry she'd literally be too petrifying. Everyone would flee in horror."
"But why is she saying that about you and the house?"
"We're scientists. She and that captive daughter of hers are raving lunatics. Just look at how they live. I don't know if she's religious or in a cult, but she seems to believe science is the issue as it conflicts with whatever she believes in—probably Satan. She phones the house sometimes and she…"
"She what?"
"Never mind."

"You can't say 'never mind' and shudder and expect that to be acceptable," I said with a snigger.
"She just says weird shit, and I know it's her because her number comes up when I do 1471. But she tries to imitate my voice. It's fucking creepy. She sounds like me."
"What does she say?"
"Just the same crap she was spitting out just then. 'Open your eyes' is the one she likes to repeat. Sometimes she just preaches Bible verses until I hang up."
I screwed up my face and rubbed my arms to rid them of the goosebumps, which Madeleine saw and said, "I know, right?"
"Have you thought of calling the police?"
"And saying what? 'The freaky woman across the road gives me the willies, can you come and tell her to leave me alone?'"
"I guess. Could you block her number?"
"That's the thing…" Madeleine stopped and held my gaze with a quivering lip. "I did." She paused, then started laughing when she saw my face. "I'm kidding! I probably could, but part of me finds it quite intriguing."

We carried on meeting other neighbours, and I tried to be enthusiastic, but I was still shaken by the encounter with the Veruschka lady. From then on, whenever she had the chance, she would heckle me from the gates. I would always speed up whenever I came to her driveway, and each time, I felt the gaze of the building following my steps. I never saw her daughter anywhere but in the window. No matter how many times I passed or what time of day, she was always there.

A few more invites were dropped into letterboxes of unanswered intercoms, then finally the last house—one Madeleine was particularly excited to visit.
"This will make you scream," she said as she pressed the bell.
"Yes?" a well-spoken older gentleman responded.
"Hello, David, it's Madeleine Magdalene."

Suddenly, Madeleine put on her posh, polite voice. The one you use for job interviews and hotel upgrades.
"Hello, Madeleine, dear! How can I help?"
"David, we're having one of our parties tomorrow night. Can you make it down?"
"If I were around, I would have said hello! Sadly, I am flying to the Amazon on Sunday. But do visit soon."
As we turned to walk back towards the house, I felt absolutely shell-shocked. "Oh my god… that was… that was David Attenborough?!"
"Yes! England's Grandad! He's literally the best bloke you'll meet. He was a guest speaker at one of my lectures, and the room ERUPTED when I announced him. You should see his collection of artefacts—it would blow your mind. He has a replica Stegosaurus endoskeleton in his conservatory. No one knows if he nicked it."
"I guess you have a thing for old fossils!"
Madeleine stopped dead, and for the first time, I saw disappointment. The trick was that humour was always the answer—but never at the expense of a national treasure.

3

The Party

There was a hive of activity outside. People were installing lights, setting up stages and sound systems, while the big band began hauling in equipment. Caterers arranged flowers and topped trays with delicious canapés as an ice sculpture was gently wheeled in and set by a man tentatively stacking champagne glasses into a pyramid. The weather was mild and warm—although contingencies had been put in place for rain—but so far, everything was perfect. Madeleine beckoned me over for the switching on of the lights. Festoon lights outlined the perimeter of the large, paved garden where the party was taking place, while smaller lights decorated the larger trees, palms, and table plants. Tiki torches were dotted around, along with gas heaters and lanterns.

"Drum roll, please!" It looked like a fairy tale. I couldn't believe everything Madeleine had envisioned had come together. It was even more lavish and phenomenal than we could have imagined.

"This is incredible! You thought this up and made it happen in less than a day! It's stunning!"

A tray of champagne was presented to us, and we shared a toast. "To new friendships!"

"To new friendships! And Libby, I love your 1920s makeup!"

"Funny story, I forgot to buy foundation—so when I asked to borrow yours, I didn't realise you wore the shade 'porcelain white.' So, this is a happy accident."

"Yeah, I don't get much sunlight in the lab, but it keeps my skin youthful."

We went upstairs to get dressed. Mad told me to take two glasses of champagne, as we needed to wait for guests to arrive before we made our entrance. Part of me worried that so much effort and expense had gone into this party that if few people showed up, it could be devastating for her. When she suggested a party, I thought of every party I'd been to in the past—usually a few cans of beer, a couple of bottles of Midori, and someone's mum's Cinzano. Every now and then, some stoners would appear with a bong, and we'd listen to Radiohead.

We made our way downstairs at around 8 p.m. The house was packed full of people! It was like something out of a film. I couldn't understand how all of this had come together so quickly, but it was everything she said it would be. I walked around, being introduced to people. Madeleine would say, "You came! You look fabulous!" if she couldn't remember their name, and she'd introduce me first, but only if she thought I might find them attractive. There must have been over two hundred people—everyone marvelling at the house and the theatrics of it all. Highlights for me included seeing Jamie Cullum playing the piano in the library, Beck doing shots with Helen Mirren, and the fire-eater being scolded by Madeleine for breathing fire too close to the ice sculpture. She decided he wouldn't be invited back.

The whole affair was like something out of *The Great Gatsby*—except everyone seemed to know Madeleine. It was my opportunity to try and pry some information out of people, to better understand who she was. The strange thing was that everyone was either a stranger or just an acquaintance and knew as little as I did—which was nothing. I knew she'd moved over from Australia not long ago, so her childhood friends would be back there—but it felt unsettling that she hadn't formed any close relationships since then. Where were her close friends? I overthought everything and had no reason not to trust her—she'd welcomed me into her home. I suppose her unwillingness to tell me about her upbringing had thrown me.

The fireworks display at 11 p.m. eclipsed any display I'd ever paid to see. People were still dancing and cavorting into the early hours. Our night ended like most others—with Mad and me curled up on the balcony under some blankets. We spent the past hour debriefing on who we'd spoken to, who said what, who wore what, and who we'd punch in the face if they couldn't remember. It was probably one of the most incredible nights of my life.
"Get used to it, kiddo," said Madeleine as she clinked my glass and sauntered off to bed.

The next morning, I awoke once more to the sound of "Jitterbug" blaring at 8 a.m. and shuddered at the thought of the clean-up operation. I wondered if people were still drinking and whether all the valuables were intact. Would there be bodies, sequins, confetti, blood, or smashed glass strewn across the lawn? It was the most peculiar feeling: I walked downstairs to the smell of coffee and freshly baked pastries. M was juicing oranges and dancing to Fleetwood Mac. I looked outside and, save for the festoon lights, which were to remain a permanent feature, everything was immaculate—not even a melted ice sculpture to complain about.
"How is it so tidy? Where did everything go? It's spotless!"
"Money," Madeleine said, cackling, "isn't it wonderful not having any responsibilities?"

Later that day, I took the train back to Oxford. M offered to drive me, but it already seemed like she'd done far too much. It felt as though this weekend had been a dream, and I needed to go back to reality and try to do some work. Two days later, still buzzing from the weekend, I was already bored to (almost literal) tears. I tried to explain to my neighbours what had happened—who I'd met and what we'd done—and even though they were all invited, they didn't believe me.
"Well, if I'd met Elton John, I'd have taken a photo. You don't have any proof."

"It really wasn't the first thing on my mind, to be honest. I was more taken aback by the fact I was discussing piano with Elton John. And proof for whom, exactly?"

From then on, in a bizarre twist, the people I had no real interest in befriending had labelled me a liar, a fantasist. Usually, I'd have reacted by inviting them to the next party, to see for themselves. Even though I was running the risk of further isolating myself, I decided I didn't need friends that badly—especially dull ones who branded me a pretender. That Thursday, we had another orchestra practice. Everyone was assigned their positions, and we played together for the first time. It sounded amazing. The talent in that room was incredibly humbling. Mad was in high spirits and was already making plans for us for the weekend, which I gratefully accepted. We hightailed it out of there, Mad peeling off the parking ticket from the windscreen and tossing it to the ground.
"You can't do that!" I declared in pure horror.
"You're right," she said, as she walked back around, picked it up, and threw it in the bin. "Littering is the devil's handiwork."

It was such a relief to get away from there. Everyone was out for themselves in some sort of contest to prove who was the wealthiest or smartest. Nate Bradbury, who I thought would be alright, turned out to be one of them. When I asked if he'd had a good weekend, he told me he'd played a game of table tennis with a guy called Wellington Hawke, who used his penis as a paddle. "He had a dick like a conger eel." I was sure not everyone was like this—of course they weren't—but it just so happened to be everyone I'd met so far. Every boy as far as the eye could see was adorned in salmon chino shorts, boat shoes, and a sweatshirt draped over their shoulders. Except for Wellington Hawke, who probably slung his ginormous eel-like appendage over his.

I won't even bother with the girls. These weren't the type of girls who befriended you; they competed with you.

This weekend, we planned next month's party—the Halloween Ball. It would be indoors this time, for no amount of money could combat the British winter. Rory and the dogs came over, as he'd had another argument with Thomas. He would usually gravitate towards Mad's house whenever they fell out, primarily to tell us how impossible Thomas was to live with, without providing one plausible reason.

Mad's plan was to replace the uplighters outside the front of the house with red bulbs, while speakers would play loops of distant crying. She would call in some favours and get ghost hunters to take a tour around the basement, during which there would be a power cut. Candelabras and the glow from the fireplace would be the only sources of light. Everyone would gather in the library, where we would play some sinister violin and cello to maintain the atmosphere. Then, fake thunder would begin to rumble from outside, stopping the music. Strobe lighting (which would appear to be lightning) would steal everyone's attention outside, where a man covered in blood would be seen staring through the window. "AND SCENE!" she bellowed, standing to take a bow.

Rory chimed in, "Isn't that a bit much, babes?"

Like most conversations with Madeleine, this one went off on a tangent. Soon, party planning was put on hold as Mad turned off the lights and started telling ghost stories. Rory was convinced their house was haunted, so he began recounting all the unexplained things they'd heard.

One night, George had been growling at the hallway, and when they went to check, there was nothing there. On inspection, a picture of Thomas's grandmother was laid face down on the bureau, and the chair that served it had been pulled out and pointed towards their bedroom. They had motion sensor lights outside and CCTV throughout, but when they reviewed the footage, there was nothing inside or out—except for a shadow passing in front of the camera, a few metres in front of George. It gave us all goosebumps. Although we completely believed Rory, he called Thomas to corroborate the story. Thomas then became freaked out and didn't want to be home alone, so he came over.

"Remembering that put the willies up me," he quipped as he walked in, picking up Michael and plopping him on his lap for support. He started smoothing Michael's head as he leant over and kissed Rory, forgetting they'd had an argument. He immediately recoiled and shifted over ever so slightly to make a point that he still wasn't forgiven. He told us another story, which he had hidden from Rory because he didn't want to frighten him. But he wasn't quite finished forgiving him yet—so he told it anyway. I shuddered. It was a bad time to realise I needed the toilet, and I was too scared to go by myself. Rory, being a gentleman, escorted me to one of the four bathrooms. As we looked to the end of the corridor, a tall female figure appeared from nowhere. We froze, like in a nightmare. I was too scared even to scream.

We clung to each other and sprinted back to the library. Thomas, surprised, exclaimed, "You two look like you've seen a ghost!" We both jabbered words at the same time, my entire body trembling. Then, the figure appeared at the door, and Rory, Thomas, and I all screamed at the top of our lungs, setting the dogs off barking. Madeleine began roaring with laughter to the point where tears were rolling down her cheeks. Then, as we composed ourselves, we realised that this was not a ghost, but an actual person.
"That's Delilah. She's working with me on a project in the lab.

"Delilah, this is Rory and Thomas from next door. Libby, you've met."
I'd not met Delilah, for I would have remembered her striking, gaunt composure. She looked like she barely existed.

We all waved and said hi, Rory bursting into a verse of "Why, why, why, Delilah?" as she stood in silence. The silence lasted an uncomfortably long time, and Rory awkwardly apologised by saying, "Sorry, we thought you were a ghost."
Delilah replied, "No problem. It happens," and then she turned, in a mechanical movement, and walked away. We all looked at each other and silently sipped our drinks until we heard the front door close.

"She's an exceptional scientist," defended Madeleine.
Rory raised an eyebrow, "She's also incredibly sinister. We should hire her for Halloween to play herself."
"Does she loosen up when you get to know her? Is she fun to work with?" I added, trying to find some positives.
"I don't employ people to be my friends! Delilah is on the verge of changing the way we receive digital information to our brains, and Jude is one of the best neurologists in the world. Together, we are creating a system that reinvents how we conceive reality. I don't really care that they're not conversationalists—in fact, I appreciate their silence."

"But are they free on Halloween?" Thomas heckled, much to Rory's amusement. "They don't even have to buy costumes; they can come as mad scientists." We all revelled in the realisation that we had a new nickname for Madeleine. All of us except Madeleine herself. Although she was exceptionally academically intelligent, she lacked common sense. It took her much longer to catch on than we'd hoped.

I changed the subject and turned to Rory and Thomas. "Do either of you have any hot, single straight friends you can invite?"

"Darling, we're gay. We're only allowed to talk to other gay men..."
There was a long pause before Thomas piped up. "Steven from Obstetrics."
"He's gay."
"Oh, really? What about John, the anaesthetist?"
"Closet gay."
"Mike from Imaging?"
"Dating Steven from Obstetrics."
Thomas turned back to me and smiled. "Sorry, darling, everyone is gay."
Madeleine stood up to pour everyone a fresh glass of wine. "I'll send invites far and wide. No uglies."

I was fuelled by a wine buzz and had the support of Rory and Thomas being there, which made me feel less awkward about asking things I shouldn't. I'd known her a week now and still had no clue how or why she was in this luxurious house and where everyone else was. I thought I'd casually ask something that would open the gates to learning more about her, her past, her family. But I got nervous and spoke before I thought, so completely out of nowhere and off-topic, I blurted out, "Why do you have such a big house?"

The room became suddenly quiet when I did so, making it appear as though I'd lost control and just shouted. Mad looked at me and smiled as she took her seat, and Rory and Thomas seemed equally intrigued. It seemed I wasn't the only one curious.

"It's my mother's brother's house. He sold a tech start-up, made millions, and enrolled my scientist father to help him with his quest to dominate space—because when you're that rich, where else is there to go other than Mars? So, he bought this house, had the most expensive lab built with the fanciest gear you'd ever seen, and it was all going fine until my dad started losing his convictions and his mind when my mum became ill. There wasn't anything wrong with her in the end, but the whole thing was weird. I thought he was drugging her to make her move back to Australia because he didn't want to carry on with the project anymore. They didn't seem to care for my opinion or input at all, and she decided to leave anyway. Eventually, he left too. The only person who stuck around was my father's business partner, Jude. I woke up one morning, and Jude broke the news to me that they'd both gone without saying goodbye. My uncle was horrified by their actions, so he gifted me the house and continues to finance all my projects, and I help him with his. And that's everything."

She could tell by the expressions on our faces that it wasn't "everything." Rory looked more horrified than when he thought he'd seen the undead. Thomas looked like he was about to cry. Wine spilled from my gaping mouth. Thomas leaned towards Mad, looking as though he was trying to touch a knee, shoulder, anything, to provide some comfort. Madeleine read the room and snapped back, "Guys, I'm not an orphan. I'm a full-grown adult, and I'm living in a mansion. Save your pity for the real victims."

It was clear she hoped that was the end of it, but there was so much to unpack. I had to know. "Have you heard from your parents since they left?"

"I haven't heard a peep in three years."

At this point, Thomas let out an audible gasp, and again Mad screwed up her face in disgust, as though we were being inappropriate.

"OK, look, they were terrible parents. Even when they were here, they weren't present. It's better this way. Their actions are reflective of their character—it's as simple as that."

"Have you tried to find them?" Thomas whispered sheepishly, hoping that the gentler he asked, the softer the response.
"Why would I try to contact them? I feel entirely ambivalent about the whole situation. Harbouring resentment just breeds more negativity, and the only way to deal with the self-absorbed is to ignore them. They don't genuinely care about my situation, only how it affects them. Do they sound like people you want to reconnect with?!"

At this point, we were just shaking our heads. The room was deadly silent as no one knew what to say. Her claims of neutrality seemed contradicted by her tone and passion. But she was angry, and she had every right to be. It was clear enough had been said that night. I offered to get some wine, but Mad stood up and said, "I'll go, that way you can talk about me when I leave the room." Except nobody said a peep. We shared a few looks. Shock, pity, concern. It felt like when you went to a friend's house as a child, and their mum started shouting at them in front of you. That feeling of inescapable awkwardness.

Later that night, after Rory and Thomas went home to their haunted mansion, Mad and I were sat playing chess. "I'm sorry your parents are arseholes."
Mad smiled and moved her rook to checkmate. "And I'm sorry that you can't defend your king."

4

October 31st, 2009 - The Halloween Ball

"Halloween has fallen on a Saturday, and there's a full moon. I'm too excited to calculate the odds of that."
Mad was in high spirits, as Brian May had just confirmed that he'd play on the balcony like he did at Buckingham Palace. "As in, the actual Brian May?"
"Yeah, curly-haired guy, in a band called Queen."
For the past few weeks, I'd spent weekdays at university—studying, reading, attending lectures, and attempting to find some interesting people (none so far)—and then spent weekends in London at Madeleine's.

Most of the time, we would get drunk, watch films, or record some tracks in the studio. Sometimes Rory and Thomas or Dan Chan and his wife would come over, but none of this led to me meeting a guy. It wasn't even about a relationship at this stage. I missed the intimacy, the feeling of lust, the nervousness of whether there'd be a kiss. Even just a gaze that turned into a mutual smile, that glimmer of possibility. By this point, Mad was becoming restless with my "perpetual whining."
"Shall I just hire you a male prostitute for the party?"
"Do you think I have to pay someone to sleep with me?"
"No, you're gorgeous. You're just very irritating, and you never take matters into your own hands. Both figuratively and literally."
"I'll make an effort to talk to someone tonight."
"Make an effort to talk to every man here until you find the right fit."
"Maybe I should have listened to you and chosen a sexier outfit than 'old witch.'"
"Yeah, about that. Your costume was destroyed. Don't ask me how. I replaced it for you. It's almost like-for-like."
It wasn't like-for-like. She pulled out a long, extremely low-cut black dress with long sleeves.

"Who is sexier than Morticia Addams? You just need to exude that same cool, smooth, sexual calmness."
"So, when people usually say to their friends 'be yourself'..."
"No, don't do that."
"You think I should dress like someone else and pretend to be someone else?"
"Only at the beginning! Pretend to have someone else's confidence. Then be yourself. Elizabeth, you've played the game before. You know there's a certain dance at the beginning. You need to get dancing. Talking of which, I got you these."
She pulled out a little brown bag that said, "Christian Louboutin." They were beautiful, classic patent black stilettos with bright red soles.
"Mad, I can't accept them. It's too much."
"If these shoes help you get laid and stop you pining, they're worth every penny. Besides, they'll look amazing and match the dress. Play me a little song later if you feel indebted."
When I reached the door, I turned back and asked, "How did my witch costume get destroyed?"
"Because I burned it."

I came back and gently wrapped my arms around her as I thanked her, and she stood rigid, like a pole. I could have hugged two of her—she was so slight. I never saw her eat. She once told me she'd developed a supplement of vitamins and fatty acids and all she needed to survive was water. Food was just for pleasure, not survival. I thought she was joking, but like most things she said, it was rarely a joke.

As before, the house looked just as she had described. The exterior walls had blood-red uplighters, and a projector lit up the entire face of the house with various horrifying ghouls. The ceilings were dripping in fake cobwebs, and small speakers lined the hallways. Rather than playful cartoon-style Halloween noises of witches cackling and ghosts chortling, these sound effects were of people screaming, crying, and distant voices yelling, "Help me." It was genuinely unsettling. I expected the Halloween song classics—"Monster Mash," "Somebody's Watching Me," "Thriller"—but no, not in Madeleine Magdalene's house. She had someone contorting the air around a theremin, a person playing the Martenot, a waterphone, a pipe organ, and a cellist. It certainly set the mood. I worried the undead would genuinely appear.

Soon, guests started arriving. Thomas bounded into the library dressed as the Phantom of the Opera. "It's so I can swoosh around in a cape and burst into song at random." Rory dressed as George Michael. Except he forgot to grow a beard in time, and he didn't anticipate the room being so dark, rendering the mirrored aviators he brought unwearable. He was just a guy in a pair of jeans and a leather jacket.

It was such an exciting time, seeing everyone's creations and the effort people had made. I only knew a handful of people in the room, but the outfits were real conversation starters. I was at the table, helping myself to another ladle of "spooky punch" when someone walked up beside me and started whispering French in my ear. My kneejerk reaction was to recoil (which I did). I turned to see a tall, handsome stranger dressed as Gomez Addams. I couldn't believe the coincidence until I remembered there are seldom coincidences in life. It was more horrifying than the theremin. I knew she was eccentric, but this was an actual stretch. It was quite funny, but also, it wasn't.
"Wow," was the only word I could initially muster.
He began trying to make conversation, but I wasn't really listening.

"I'm absolutely speechless," I began.
"I know, it's such a coincidence that—" (I cut him off.)
"I mean, surely it's a joke. What did Mad tell you to do exactly?"
"Um, just show up at 7 p.m., wear a costume. It was on the invitation that I—" (I cut him off again.)
"Should wear a Gomez costume. Do I look like the type of woman who needs to pay for sex?"
He stared at me with a deep seriousness, not breaking character as Gomez.
"Um, no... no, you don't. Sorry, what?"
"I'm curious, how much did Madeleine pay you for this evening? How much do you usually charge?"
"I just de—"
"You know what, don't answer that. All the handsome guys are either gay or prostitutes."
I stormed off to find M. She was standing by the door talking with Dan Chan, debating whether lacing the punch with acid was a step too far.
"M, I can't believe you would do this to me!"
"Libby! Drink more and relax into it—you look incredible!"
"I'm talking about the gentleman of the night you employed to have sex with me."
She spat out her drink, allowing it to land on herself rather than her priceless, vintage rug.
"What the fuck are you talking about?!" she stammered out between laughter.
"You got me a man-whore."
She continued laughing uncontrollably before composing herself to ask, "Whence is this gigolo?"
"That fucking guy! Gomez fucking Addams."
I pointed over at a bewildered-looking Gomez, still standing by the punch.
"Oh, Liberace, you poor lamb. He's the graphic designer. The son of my family's friends."

Madeleine went over to talk to him. I tried not to look, but I couldn't help myself. He pointed to himself, looked confused, and then looked up to see me staring at him. Mad then began trying to beckon me over. I shook my head vigorously. I would brave the terrifying hallway and escape to the kitchen for a cigarette rather than face up to that shitstorm. Rory and Thomas were already in there, carving up some lines of cocaine and flirting with a very stacked Zeus, who, although "wasn't gay," was showing them how many push-ups he could do in a toga.

"Lib, I didn't know you smoked?" said Rory, extending a Marlboro Light from its sheath.

"I do today!"

I told them what had happened, and they shrugged, as though this happened to them all the time. Rory lifted his head from the table and in his nonchalant, sarcastic voice, piped up, "Just tell him it was an easy mistake because he looks like a cheap whore."

Thomas slapped Rory's shoulder and gave me a hug. "Don't catastrophise, Lizzy. Try to see the funny side. Have another drink."

"I asked him if I looked like the type of woman who should pay for sex."

Right then, Gomez appeared at the door, smirking like a naughty schoolboy. He came over to start teasing me. I considered running out the back door, because that was my nature—to run from situations where I felt compromised or embarrassed. This was exactly the pattern I had to break. Rory, Thomas, and Zeus all sloped off together, Rory winking at me as Thomas shoved him out of the room. Gomez introduced himself properly, adding, "I'm not a prostitute, but if you want to pay me for the night, you're more than welcome."

He was incredibly cocky, which I usually found off-putting, but there was something unspeakably compelling about him. I knew he was trouble, and I knew he was saying things he thought I wanted to hear. But he made me laugh. I felt comfortable around him, mainly because he did most of the talking, and his confidence more than made up for the two of us. I flirted back, whatever that means, and I did what I usually do in these situations—drank in excess to bury the nerves. We sat in the kitchen, enjoying watching people walk in for a line of coke and then look confused, pretending they'd got the wrong room. We played "guess the name of the guest," as neither of us knew anyone, and we had to call out a name as they left to see if they would turn around. When Gomez guessed "Richard," we high-fived. It felt so easy to talk to him. We laughed, smoked, and drank some punch before an angry little succubus named Madeleine Magdalene summoned us to the library. "You're holding up the fucking spook show!" she shouted, with a glare that didn't quit. "Hurry the fuck up." It was the scariest thing we'd seen all night.

We walked towards the library as terrifying effigies fell from hidden crevices in the hallway. Once we arrived, the power was cut within seconds. The thunder clapped on cue, and everyone looked towards the window as the faux lightning lit up the silhouette of a terrifying chainsaw murderer. At least that's what I gather everyone saw. As soon as the lights went out, my fictional husband reached out and pulled me towards him, pretending to protect me from the darkness. I'm not sure if it was the punch, the dress, or the embodiment of Morticia, but I reciprocated with a kiss.

At the same time as the blood-covered, power-tool-wielding maniac appeared at the window, Caroline Ingleman from four doors down started screaming and screaming and screaming. Madeleine caught Dan Chan's worried glare across the room, and they nodded in unison—yes, they had put too much acid in the punch.

An hour passed. Gomez and I were still going strong. Unusually for me, I couldn't stop talking. I was enthusiastic and tactile even. I excused myself to go to the toilet and bumped into Mad and Rory. Rory held my chin and stared into my eyes. "How much punch have you had, dear?"
"Four, five, six glasses. I'm having the best night!"
"Darling, your pupils are the size of golf balls. You're as high as the Space Station."
Madeleine had forgotten to tell me she'd spiked the punch. And believe it or not, this wouldn't be the last time she accidentally drugged me. I looked down and saw I was stroking Rory's unusually furry hands without even realising.
"You have hands like a ferret."
"Madeleine!" he shouted. "You've broken Elizabeth!"

The rest of the night was a blur. The next morning—although technically, it was past noon by the time I woke up—I found myself alone. I got up to close the curtains, squinting as the sunlight burned like a vampire's worst nightmare. Standing up turned out to be a mistake; my head pounded, and my mouth was unbearably dry. Anxiety gnawed at me so intensely that I had to gather the courage just to get a glass of water. I was still dressed, alone, and, despite everything, I didn't get the impression the night had been a total disaster. I remembered laughing uncontrollably at one point, being terrified of the carpet at another. In fact, the last thing I recall was gasping in fear after forgetting that the sound effects weren't real. Gomez had started shouting, "The walls are screaming! The walls are screaming!" That's when I ran up here to hide under the covers—and I had some vague memory that Gomez had come with me.

I looked at my phone, but the screen brightness almost blinded me. No messages from him. It looked as though I'd tried to save his number, but I'd only managed "GOnr-999;153-(98." I did have a voicemail from Rory, sent at 2:33 a.m.: "Elizabeth, I nearly died falling off a cliff," followed by crying before he hung up.

A horrible feeling settled in my stomach. Had I embarrassed myself? I was still wearing everything from the night before, apart from my shoes, which I remembered taking off when they mutated into snakes. I hoped Gomez was in just as much of a state. Mad texted me his number, and I messaged him, asking if he was alive. He replied, "barely." I didn't hear from him for two days after that, so I decided to initiate the conversation. Looking back, I realised I had to initiate all the conversations; I was always the one arranging a "date." And I use that term loosely since we never went on a "proper date." For reasons I learned later, he would only ever come to my house. It looks ridiculous now in hindsight. You know in your gut it doesn't feel right, yet you stay hopeful. Mad always said, "If you're getting mixed messages, he's not into you." She dispensed that advice suspiciously freely for someone who had never been in a relationship.

The issue with Gomez was that it was never the right time—for him, anyway. Over the next few years, there would be an endless cycle of unrequited feelings based solely on the fact that he just didn't care. Even when he was in relationships with other people, I was the emergency key kept under the stone. Occasionally useful, but mostly just there as a comfort in case of emergencies.

5

18th December 2009

A round of applause filled the theatre as we stood to take a bow. The end-of-year Christmas performance was over, and we all grabbed our winter coats to head to The King's Arms for mulled wine. I had never seen Mad so animated. She wore her Christmas jumper with pride, jangly silver snowman earrings, and cream fluffy earmuffs on top of her woolly hat. She really hadn't been lying when she said she loved Christmas! On 15th November—much sooner than most—she began enshrouding the house in Christmas decorations and lights. Tasteful but plentiful. Every weekend was spent carol singing, making eggnog, eating mince pies in front of the fire, and watching all the classic films.

Around 10 p.m., Mad asked if I wanted to go to Winter Wonderland tomorrow. I said I was planning to get the train home in the morning but could take my suitcase to hers and leave straight after. Her face fell, then contorted into an unnatural, overly compensatory smile. She hadn't realised I'd be going home to see my family. We'd spent the last three months almost inseparably, save for my classes. I immediately felt awful, realising her favourite time of year would be spent alone. "You could come with me? To Devon? You can spend Christmas with us?" Her bottom lip unconsciously enveloped the other, and when she realised she was pouting, she snapped herself out of it.

"Don't be silly—I'm not going to intrude! Most years, I go to Rory and Thomas's for lunch. It's great fun. Thomas cooks, we all drink. The dogs get a walk, then we watch the Queen's speech. We sometimes take an E and then pass out."

The next morning, Madeleine's dispiritedness disappeared as soon as she started prancing through the Christmas market. She bought trinkets, drank Glühwein, and stashed warm chestnuts in her pockets like a gerbil. We sat atop the Ferris wheel, gazing down at the merry crowd below, and I decided then that I wouldn't go home. I sent a message to both my parents, which was met with slight sadness from my mother, mainly because "Your father probably won't bother with a tree now." I broke the news to Mad while we queued for candyfloss, and she smiled for so long I worried her teeth would freeze.

She pointed towards The Dorchester. "This changes everything! We'll start with cocktails—then we need to go to the Food Hall. We'll prepare a feast for Christmas Day and dine like kings!"

When I suggested we could now host a New Year's Eve party, she almost melted into the pavement. As we walked through the foyer, a sudden jolt of panic hit me when I saw the floor-to-ceiling Christmas tree with a bundle of presents beneath it. I'd only bought Madeleine a small novelty gift. The ante had been upped now that I was staying for Christmas, and I needed to be creative—especially since my bank balance currently had only two digits. As we sat in the luxurious bar on velvet chairs, I was distracted by thoughts of what to get her. And then, as if by magic, the universe decided to help.

Madeleine leapt up like a rocket launch, sending her bar stool crashing to the ground. Panicked, I turned to see what had caused her to flee so dramatically—a puppy hanging out of an elegant lady's handbag. Instinctively, I knew what to do. I asked for the bill, and four cocktails (six sips each) later, my account was drained.

I told Mad to drink up as we needed to be somewhere. Her sheer delight that I wouldn't tell her where we were going! She didn't even seem too disheartened when we started descending the Tube escalators. Two changes, a toilet break, and a beer stop later, we arrived at Battersea Dogs Home. I hadn't anticipated how emotional it would be. This trip gave us two things: a four-year-old springer spaniel called Bingo, and a concept for our New Year's Eve party.

Tears streamed from Mad's eyes as she saw all the unwanted dogs lying sadly in their cages. I had to hold her shoulders at one point and explain that we couldn't "take them all home" just because she had the money and the space. Many of these dogs weren't ready to be integrated with other dogs—they needed time, love, and training as well as a home. I pointed to the information printed on the top right of each cage, which outlined the behaviour issues and ideal home environments for each dog. "But we can't just leave them here," she blubbered, her lip trembling. I thought I had made a grievous error, until we came up with the idea of having a fundraiser. Mad would invite all her wealthy friends and contacts to either adopt or sponsor a dog. By New Year, we would make sure each of these pups either had a home or the rehabilitation they needed.

I was worried it would be hard for her to narrow down her choice. All the dogs came up to greet her as we passed, looking longingly for a home—except Bingo. He walked up to us, and as we crouched down and began making kissing noises, he looked at us with disdain before turning away and heading back to his bed. "Oh my God, that one," she cried. "What an absolute diva. Did you see the way he dissed me?" When Bingo was let out of his kennel, he was even more like Madeleine than we'd realised. As she fussed over his chin, he turned his eyes away as if disinterested, but his little tail started tapping the floor uncontrollably. He tried to hide his feelings. I wished then that Madeleine had a tail—it would make her emotions a lot clearer.

They filled out the paperwork while I put all the necessary dog supplies on my credit card. I'd have time to get some extra dog-related gifts by Christmas Day. They ran out together like competitors at Crufts.

"He's the best present I've ever had. I love him. This will be the best Christmas ever! But don't ever make me take public transport again. Ever. Not all those tears were for the puppies." I leaned in to hug her, telling her she was welcome, and she looked away, saying, "Too much." But the tail was wagging.

Bingo soon became our best friend. We had to line the entrance hall with puppy pads because when I came over at weekends, he'd get so excited he'd have a little accident by the door. He slept on Mad's bed, followed her everywhere, and spent his mornings chasing squirrels and his afternoons flushing game.

The Christmas Dog Rehabilitation Ball

It made the previous gatherings look like a practice run. News of the past two parties had spread far and wide, and when rumours of a Christmas soiree began circulating, people were begging friends of friends for an invite. Musicians, actors, models, moguls—all sorts of riffraff were reaching out for a coveted golden envelope.

Every invite received an RSVP of "Yes," apart from one: the ever-unreliable Gomez. It had been two weeks since I'd seen him and days since we'd spoken. He gave me a half-hearted, "If I'm not too tired after work drinks, I'll try and make it."

"He's not coming. Meet someone else," Mad cried as she stapled another mistletoe to a doorframe. Although I knew he probably wouldn't come, I remained optimistic that, as it was Christmas—like in every romantic Christmas film—he'd turn up at the end of the night when I was sitting alone feeling sad, making a grand entrance and an even bigger gesture. My eyes would light up like the North Star, and we'd kiss under one of the fifteen mistletoes Mad had planted around the house. I'll save you the suspense: he didn't come. No appearance, no apology, not even a message. Every time someone walked through the door, I'd hold my breath, thinking it was him. I wasn't the first girl to be foolish, and I wouldn't be the last.

My sadness at spending the last of my credit card balance on a rather remarkable red Christmas dress was short-lived. After all, I looked better than my usual "passable" self, and we spent the first part of our evening helping rehome all the animals. Although the dogs weren't in attendance (for several reasons), we managed to find homes for twenty-five dogs (twenty were successful) and raised a lot of money to help the others. There was also a generous donation from an anonymous benefactor, whom we all knew was Madeleine.

By around 11 p.m., I was doing shots of "Christmas Nipples"* with the Chans and trying to figure out how Mad had managed to arrange a reindeer enclosure. "Attenborough must have had something to do with this," joked Thomas, standing with heart-shaped eyes, cooing over the winter wonderland. But that night wouldn't be remembered for reindeer, a fountain of eggnog, or a full choir belting out carols. Nor for my blind infatuation with a man who wasn't interested. It was the night we met our new lodger.

*Christmas Nipples: eggnog, Baileys, butterscotch schnapps (it's a rich number).

John's taxi, like every other taxi that deposited a passenger on our street, had really only come to bring someone to Madeleine's house. None of the other property names were visible, let alone numbered. As John stepped out of the car and began walking towards Mad's mansion in all its illuminated glory, he realised this wasn't the right house. When he heard piano music gently escaping the two-inch-thick front door, he turned to walk away. Luckily for him, Madeleine had glimpsed the startlingly good-looking stranger as she came back from fetching a bottle of Pétrus from her private vault. She flung the door open, and before he had a chance to speak, Madeleine took his arm and dragged him inside. He was older than us, maybe late twenties, or mid-thirties (we never knew), tall, well-dressed in a polo shirt and sports jacket, with dark troubled brown eyes and mousy hair. He had an impatient energy about him. His eyes darted about, taking in his surroundings with nervous speed.

Mad didn't even pause to ask for his name as she led him through to the ballroom. John wasn't one for emotions or reactions, but he was visibly impressed by the grandiosity of it all. She kept talking at him, his first utterance being "sure" when she offered him a glass of champagne from a passing tray. He tentatively listened to Mad's ramblings as he scanned the room, noting every guest, every window, every exit. Mad then invited him to step outside to see the rest of the Christmas display. Like a working dog that's just heard a pheasant, John handed Mad his drink and began sprinting towards the eastern boundary fence. Despite the party noise, John heard the distinct sound of nearby gunfire. The safe house next door, the one he was supposed to be holing up in, had just been compromised.

He'd suspected there was a leak for a while but hadn't realised it was one of his team. He ran back to Madeleine, ushering her indoors almost as urgently as she'd dragged him in earlier. He explained, with as little detail as necessary, that he was in MI5, supposed to be next door, and that it had been attacked. His concern was that they would be targeted. Mad, of course, thought he was an actor hired by one of us (probably Rory) as a Christmas gag. She cooperated, laughing her head off and saluting him as he ordered her to keep everyone secure in the ballroom. "Aye aye, Captain, mum's the word," she whispered, winking as she closed the doors. She turned to the nearest person. "He's fantastic. We should have him at every party."

John cautiously slipped out of the door and softly tiptoed around the topiary hedges, careful not to step on the crunchy stones. He heard as the men next door ran to the car with its engine running in the street. Two doors slammed, and the vehicle screeched away. He took the battery and SIM card from his burner phone, smashed both with the butt of his gun, and tossed the remains into the safe house garden. From the shadows atop the carport, he watched and waited—only ten or fifteen minutes—until the cleaning team arrived. He observed, gauging their reactions, primarily to check if they'd consider that he could be next door.

When they restored power to the safe house, he saw two of the agents lying dead through the downstairs window. His closest confidant, Louis, leant down to pick up the remnants of the destroyed mobile. He stood and looked around briefly, but assumed John was long gone by now, which historically would be the case. John inspected Louis's face for signs of complicity, hoping he was making a grievous mistake. He saw neither surprise nor concern. Around two hours later, everyone left. John knew nobody would suspect him of being next door, and that it was probably the best place for him to lie low. Borderline hypothermic, he tapped on the front door and was soon met by Thomas's enthusiastic smile, letting him in without question.

John sat down with Mad, who'd already forgotten who he was as she started talking at him again. She told him he could stay as long as he needed. She didn't remember this conversation—or even him—in the morning. From that moment on, John stayed with us, Mad always assuming he was a friend of mine, never questioning his presence. The day he left, when he extended his gratitude, Mad was completely unaware of any of their conversations about his reason for being there or his profession. It was news to her upon his exit that he was even a spy—although I'd had my suspicions.

On 16th January, he was walking down the corridor as I flung open the bathroom door. Without thinking, he tried to get me into a headlock before his split-second reflexes stopped him. Not before catching his watch on my towel, which left me scrambling naked on the floor. I was about to say he was deeply apologetic, but now that I think of it, he wasn't. He was almost angry at me for being in his way.

I imagine we would have spoken more about his rather truculent attitude if it weren't for the fact that he didn't have any clothes, so when he did laundry, he walked around topless. Mad and I were in the lounge the first time it happened. He walked past, and we silently caught each other's eye—my mouth agape, Mad mouthing, "Holy shit." His bedroom door was mostly closed, apart from one time when it was ajar, and I peeped in to see him in a handstand doing push-ups. I must have gulped audibly because he flipped back to a standing position and looked towards the door. I scurried back to my room like a naughty child. My heart was pounding. The thought of walking down the corridor and into John's room late at night became an ongoing obsession.

I made the mistake of telling Mad I thought he was attractive. "Just go to his room and ask if he wants to bosh," was her response. I begged her not to say anything. I was immediately terrified she would, but thankfully she didn't. Once, when we'd had a few drinks, I hovered outside his room before chuckling to myself. As if. Imagine having the nerve to be that brazen and then being rejected, having to see him every day afterwards. The thought alone made me shiver.

On 3rd February, I had an insatiable thirst, so I stood in my pyjamas, staring into the fridge. Mad and I had stayed up drinking some foul old bourbon and playing poker until 2 a.m. I saw orange juice and began glugging it unapologetically straight from the carton, the contents not all going in my mouth. I saw John approaching from the corner of my eye, and suddenly, he grabbed me from behind and dragged me down towards the ground, his back against the kitchen island facing the door he'd come in from. One arm wrapped around my waist, his other hand covering my mouth, which still contained a gulp of orange juice. I was almost too afraid to swallow. "Don't say a word," he whispered in my ear. "Someone out there has a gun." I looked up at the mirror. For some reason, I whispered back instead of speaking normally, "That's the gardener, Nick. He's jet-washing the patio. That's a pressure washer nozzle." John released his grip, and again, I'd love to say he apologised, but he didn't.

Instead of a normal reaction—thinking, "That man's insane, why would he think Nick had a gun?"—I just felt oddly turned on by the whole thing. I mean, he thought someone had a gun, and the first thing he wanted to do was save my life. What's not to like? He pulled us both up, switched on the kettle, satisfied we were no longer under attack, and started whistling the theme tune to *Some Mothers Do 'Ave 'Em. *

I messaged Gomez to tell him what happened. That seemed to be our only form of communication, despite him living ten minutes down the road. We'd become pen pals who occasionally hooked up. Sometimes he'd call, and we'd talk for hours. One thing he never had a problem with was talking nonsense. "He wants to sleep with you. What a creative excuse to feel someone up before breakfast."

"It didn't feel sexual. It felt like he was genuinely paranoid." That was when I first thought maybe we should find out more about the stranger living with us. He'd been here for two months, and if he wanted us dead, he was certainly playing the long game. I gathered he was hiding from someone. If anything, I thought he was a criminal on the run. He didn't seem like a spy. But I guess that's the point—they're not supposed to be obvious. John always looked angry, worn out, run down, and hurt by everyone in his past. He didn't have any warmth, and certainly didn't respond to anyone offering him any.

"He literally sounds like a psychopath," said Gomez. The thing that bothered me most about this conversation wasn't that Gomez was right, but that he didn't seem bothered or jealous. He hadn't even met John, despite coming over multiple times. I'd told him we thought John was gorgeous, and he was genuinely unfazed. I wanted him so badly to like me. I guess that's why I let it go on as long as it did.

10th February

A few of us were having gin and playing games for Dan’s birthday. I snuck out to the kitchen for a sneaky cigarette with Rory, and we stood by the back door, opening it to exhale as it was too cold to stand outside. We heard a commotion coming from outside the lab, and Rory put his finger to his lips so we could eavesdrop. It was Delilah and Jude. "This isn’t right," said Delilah. "I don’t agree with the way you’re going about this." We eagerly awaited the reply, but it was mostly garbled; the only words we could hear clearly were, "All of this is for the sake of discovery. Madeleine will appreciate that, and so should you." It sounded like the argument was dissipating, so we tried to slope away like mice, pretending we’d never been there. Jude sniffed as he walked past, pausing to notice the scent of tobacco. We held our breath, exhaling only when his footsteps faded. We walked slowly back to the party, harbouring the uncertainty of a half-heard conversation when the wall phone rang as we passed, sending us both into a startled stupor. I held up the receiver so we could both hear as Mrs Veruschka started mimicking Madeleine: "Open your eyes. Open your eyes." I replaced the receiver on the wall, and Rory was shocked. "It sounds just like her. That’s really unsettling."

"Isn’t it just."

February 11th

Someone was at the door. I was sitting, reading coursework with Bingo on my lap, who leapt up and started barking before they even had the chance to ring the doorbell. I kept shushing him as we walked towards the entrance. The ceilings were so high that each bark echoed like a church bell. It was Jude again. He hadn't met Bingo before, and as soon as I opened the door, Bingo continued to bark, louder than I'd ever heard. Jude stepped back, his eyes flashing with irritation. "That dog is vicious. That's why you should never get them from a shelter."
"Bingo is the most gentle, submissive dog! He literally loves everyone." Except Jude. I held his collar, trying to soothe him. The barking stopped, but Bingo wouldn't stop growling. I'd never seen him like this before. "Did you want to come in? I can put Bingo in the library."
Jude didn't respond. He just stepped away, walking around the side of the house to access the lab from there.

Later that night, when Mad came over for a cocktail, I told her what had happened. She teasingly called Bingo a "furry little psycho" but quickly sprang to Jude's defence. "There must be a reason," she said, stroking Bingo's ears. "Either Jude, Bingo, or both had an experience when they were younger that's triggered this. It has to be some kind of past ordeal. Why does Jude never come inside, by the way? He always comes over, but he never enters."
"Maybe bad memories from when he worked with my father. They were all remarkably close. Some people find it hard to return to the site of trauma. Why do you never go back to University Halls?" she teased, as she began pouring two glasses of the blue cocktail she'd been working on.
"But Rory and I heard him and Delilah arguing last night," I continued.
"They always argue. They disagree over everything because they work in diverse ways.. He's old school."
Her protection of his character was indomitable. She was as unwaveringly believing in him as I was in Gomez.

Valentine's Day

It had been quite a while since I'd been back to Oxford. After a long, drunken conversation with Mad on Rory's birthday, she convinced me to retrieve my belongings and move in with her. It didn't take much persuading; I left only the essentials back in Oxford, figuring I couldn't skip every lecture. Could I? When I initially resisted her suggestion, she pointed me to a paper on my reading list. She'd written it. "Read that stack of books, and I'll give you my notes. You can complete your assignments and spend the rest of the term playing music, sipping coffee, reading, travelling, LIVING." You can't argue with a genius.

By now, we had a routine. I'd wake up every morning at 8 to her alarm. She'd be in the kitchen, brewing coffee, drinking orange juice, and listening to Fleetwood Mac. There were always pastries, though I was never sure where they came from, and I never saw her eat one. I'd sit with her while she ranted about the news, her brow furrowed in disapproval. We'd usually spend the first hours of the day debating her curmudgeonly outlook. Sometimes, if the mood were right, we'd end up playing music or planning our next party. Sometimes she'd be dressed in some whimsical outfit for the day's event. "We're clay pigeon shooting at 1pm!", as she stood in full hunting regalia. Once, she brought in a rotating whiteboard on wheels, covered in wild suggestions for entertainment and guest lists—my favourite being "Stevie Nicks/Lindsey Buckingham (are they speaking yet?)." Whenever I sneered, she'd say, "Aim low, Elizabeth, and that's where you'll end up."

Today was different.

Her alarm went off at 8 a.m., playing "Jitterbug" as usual. Was that Mad laughing? Not just laughing, but giggling. I checked the grandfather clock at the foot of the stairs: only 9:30 a.m. Too early for a mimosa. She was perched on the breakfast bar, her legs swinging, her eyes sparkling as she flirted with a male visitor. He was handsome, with floppy black hair that he kept pushing back over his forehead, barefoot and wearing rainbow tie-dyed pyjamas with a balalaika strapped to his back. He danced around like a court jester, and she seemed utterly entranced.

"Huzzah!" he cried when he noticed me. The eccentric fellow scuttled over and threw his arms around me as though we were old friends. "Madeleine has told me so much about you!" Yet I'd heard nothing about him. I'd heard nothing about any of Mad's friends, actually.

With an unusually bright grin, Mad introduced him as Lucas. "He's a nomad, a musical genius—the next Mozart," she said. He'd just been travelling through Russia with a band he'd met in an Irish bar. It was like he'd stepped out of 1965 by accident. He looked young—maybe eighteen, but he could have been twenty-seven for all I knew. He told me his mum was Cantonese, giving him "the skin of eternal youth." Lucas was her first boyfriend, and I got the sense that if he weren't such a free spirit, he might have been her last. He suddenly saw something in the garden, and with a playful gesture, pulled Mad down to chase it. Just like Bingo when he saw a squirrel. Was Madeleine… skipping? Then Lucas stopped by a tree, swung his balalaika around, and started singing to her. And she didn't hate it. She looked like she might cry. Everything I thought I knew about her—her nonchalance towards men, her resistance to romance—was all wrong. She wasn't disinterested; they just weren't Lucas.

They spent the day running around like children. Occasionally they'd stop, kiss, smile, and carry on. I'd never seen this side of Mad; it was as if Lucas had awoken something in her, a light buried under years of debris. When we went to the studio, as each fluorescent light flickered on, Lucas's eyes grew wider. It was as if Mad had unveiled a lost priceless plunder. He moved through the room with the ease and speed of a child in soft play, touching and playing every instrument.

"Does he have ADHD?" I asked.
"Would you like him any less if he did?" she replied, defensive. I stammered an apology. "Then don't ask," she said, turning away. She walked over to join Lucas, her frown turning to a smile. She gestured for me to join them. "Lib—show him what you can do on the piano."

Playing together was novel and vibrant. I could see why Mad liked him; he played every instrument effortlessly. He stood over me, strumming a Gibson, nodding along to my improvisation. "Here, try this," he said, flinging the guitar over his shoulder and taking my place at the piano, playing my tune—but better. Painfully better. I'd spent my life trying to master one instrument, and here was this man in rainbow pyjamas, a master of everything.

As I watched Lucas, his energy infectious, I realised he wasn't who I'd imagined for her. I never pictured her with anyone, really. She always seemed apathetic to the idea. But here she was, undeniably in love. And it struck me—I didn't really know her at all. I decided to get to know Lucas better, if I could ever get him to sit still.

We had drinks and charcuterie instead of dinner. Lucas was just as skilled in the kitchen as the studio. Mad was upstairs, "getting ready"—a shock, considering she'd spent most of January in pyjamas and a messy bun.

"She talks about you all the time," Lucas said as he whipped up houmous. "You're more of a sister to her than her real sister."
"She has a sister?"
"Didn't get on with her much. Her sister was the family's 'success story'—not that she'd actually succeeded at anything." He made a face, tasting the houmous. "She stayed in Australia when the family moved here. Caused a rift, I think."
"How long have you known Mad?"
"Since school. We've been best friends since we could talk. She's brilliant—so smart, so beautiful. Such a breath of fresh air."

I smiled, taking a sip of wine, trying not to spill it as I chuckled. "To be honest, Lucas, your arrival is the most jovial I've ever seen her."

"Really?" He seemed surprised. "She said having you around has made her the happiest she's ever felt. You've woken something in her. You're her muse. I've never seen anyone play piano as well as her, until I met you."
"Wait, she plays the piano?"
"Plays everything. But violin's her passion."
She'd never played around me. Probably didn't want to embarrass me. I was sure she'd be better.

Mad appeared at the door, wearing a black jumper dress, her hair loose and swept to one side, make-up on—a rare occurrence. She'd set out the good china in the dining room, the fire lit, candelabras on the table. We stayed up late, listening to Lucas tell stories of his travels, singing for his supper. He spoke of touring the world, playing with the best musicians, eating local foods, drinking with natives, and sleeping under the stars. A carefree life. At the end of the night, he carried Mad upstairs, both giggling. I had another glass of wine alone, checking my phone for a message from Gomez. Nothing. Midnight came, and I blew out the candles, a little teary as each flame turned to smoke. By morning, Lucas was gone.

I came downstairs to find Mad drinking her orange juice. No coffee, no Fleetwood Mac, no pastries, no Lucas. Like a Valentine's ghost, he'd appeared to bring joy, then vanished, taking her smile with him. Even I felt sad. "A rolling stone gathers no moss," Mad said, rereading the same paragraph of the paper. "Are you all right?" I asked, feeling foolish. "Yes, of course. It's just Lucas. He'll be back." She felt my gaze and lowered the broadsheet. "What?" she snapped. It was the first time I'd heard her lose her patience. "Don't worry, Lizard. He'll come back. And one day we'll get married. We've made a pact. It's why no one else is good enough." She folded the paper and finished her drink. She headed to the lab, and I didn't see her for weeks. That evening, I took her a plate of food and knocked on the door, but the next morning it was still there. Her alarm still sounded at 8 a.m., but for a month, the music stopped.

7

April 20th, 2009

Madeleine was hardly seen after Lucas left. I spent my time studying, picking daffodils from the garden, brightening the house. Apart from the occasional shuffle of the maintenance staff, it was just me. When the doorbell finally rang, I was relieved. It was Jude. "Come in!" I offered, a bit too enthusiastically. "Mad's in the lab." He hesitated, staring at the threshold like a vampire needing an invitation. "The side gate's locked," he said irritably. "Want me to get her?" He looked at me, then turned away. "I'll come back later." He already had a foot in his car when I called out, "Why don't you like me?" He paused. "I don't dislike you, Elizabeth. You hold Madeleine back, which holds me back." He shut the door and drove off.

After that, I decided to rescue my friend. Was Jude suggesting she was just a commodity to him? Was that why he came here? To exploit her intelligence? After five minutes of knocking (and Bingo's excited barking), she opened the door. She looked tired, worn out. "What month is it?" she asked, as if time didn't exist in the lab. "April," I replied, concerned.
"That's all right then. Are you okay?" She asked, remembering that life still continued without her. "I'm fine. I was just worried you'd forgotten to live."
"I'm a bad friend. Let me finish here, and we'll hang out."

She resurfaced to the garden, shielding her eyes from the sun. I sat at the table, doodling. She returned wearing sunglasses, brandishing two glasses and a bottle of Sancerre. "So, what have you been working on while I've been trying to crack the Big Bang, Miss Elizabeth?"

"I've made some life-changing discoveries of my own," I said, passing her my sketchbook. "It's called 'Rats for Dinner'—an illustrated book about a group of intellectually evolved rats living in a disused tube station. They're trying to integrate into society but are unsure if they want to. They gather for dinner to discuss their place in the world." I waited for Mad to scold me for wasting time, but instead, she looked genuinely awestruck.

"This is brilliant," she said. "The rats represent so many societal groups afraid to come to the surface. And your drawings—who knew you could draw like this?"
"I always wanted to be an artist. My parents discouraged it. 'Focus on piano!' they'd say."
"Tell that to Van Gogh, Monet, Vermeer."
"They all died penniless, thinking they were failures."
"As will you if you keep that attitude."
"Van Gogh shot himself in the chest. He was only celebrated posthumously."
"You need to finish this. Complete the narrative—figure out the rats' future. This is 'Animal Farm' for the sewers!"
"I'm struggling with the story. I only got as far as the illustrations."
"Then let me help," Mad said, pulling out a notebook, seemingly from nowhere. "Allow me to be the Dahl to your Blake."

We spent the rest of the night plotting our rat novella. But, like most things I started, it went into my box of unfinished projects.

May 2010

Mad was leaving that morning to go to Los Angeles. If I didn't have a bunch of exams, I would have gone in a heartbeat. I invited Gomez over at the last minute, and, remarkably, he said yes. We'd averaged meeting up about once a month, with nothing progressing beyond friends who slept together. The weather was gorgeous, and I woke up feeling confident and excited. Music pumped out downstairs as I studied various YouTube videos on traditional lasagne. I put the beef ragu on to slow cook through the day, while I went for a long walk with Bingo on the Heath. I spent about two hours getting ready that afternoon, opting for a casual white shirt and denim skirt. I didn't want to look like I'd tried too hard; I wanted to seem as though I'd just thrown this on and not spent the whole day obsessing about it.

I looked at the clock—Gomez would be here in an hour. I slowly finished the rest of the red wine that I'd put in the ragu while topping up my makeup, then put on the "Moon Safari" album by Air and opened all the French windows (before realising it wasn't that warm) and immediately closing them. I wanted this to be more of a date, rather than just us having sex. I had to break this pattern if there was any chance of it becoming something more. For people who spoke so often, we didn't really know anything about each other.

It started positively. He walked in smiling and gave me a kiss, saying, "Look at you," as he sauntered past, looking me up and down. I walked towards the kitchen, and he paused at the bottom of the staircase and said, "We should take this upstairs, young lady," in a comical voice. I smiled, then continued to the kitchen. "Follow me, there's a surprise." He made an 'ooooooo' sound and started rubbing his hands together. "Ta-da!" I said, pointing to the table, which held the bruschetta I'd made as a starter, along with two large Aperol Spritzes. "I thought we could go to Italy!" I pressed play with the remote control, and "That's Amore" started filling the room. Gomez wasn't giving me the reaction I'd hoped for when I imagined this evening in my head—especially when he told me that he was meeting all his family and friends for dinner in an hour. "I'm sorry you went to all this effort, but I've only got an hour." He then stared down at my laptop, which was open on the worktop, and read out, "[The Sound of the Soul: The Philosophy and Psychology of Music]—is this your book?" I nodded. "What an absolute geek," he said before laughing. He wrapped his hands around my waist and tried to kiss me. I did not feel like reciprocating much, given that all he'd done since arriving was insult me.

"I assumed that when you said you'd be over at 6 p.m., you wouldn't have eaten. You never said you had plans after, or else I would have..."

I stopped there. I was such a fool. He'd set aside an hour to come and hook up with me before going to spend time with the people that really mattered. Then it dawned on me. "How come you're meeting all your family and friends? Is it your birthday?"

This was when he told me he was moving to Edinburgh for work. Next week. This wasn't something he'd mentioned in any of our conversations before. "I thought this was just a bit of fun," he continued, which was the part that really crushed me. Not to mention that all his friends were going, which meant I didn't even rank as a friend.

"Why? Why are you moving to Edinburgh? How long have you known?" He said nothing apart from a limp, "Libby," as he moved in to try and touch me again.

I just shook my head as I realised, "You've known the whole time."

"Which is why I didn't want to lead you on."

"Not telling me you were leaving at any point—that was leading me on."

I wasn't having fun anymore. I didn't know how to handle it. I'd never encountered anything so heartless before. He delivered everything in such a matter-of-fact way. There was no feeling in his eyes. "You should probably go. You don't want to keep your friends waiting."

He reached over to hold my shoulders, so I turned and started walking towards the front door, trying my hardest not to cry. I was overcome with a cocktail of anger and sadness, mainly directed at myself for being so naïve. I managed to usher him out of the door, and after I closed it, he knocked a couple of times before deciding to walk away, making the minimal effort. I hadn't felt this way before. I was so annoyed. I was such an absolute idiot, and then simultaneously, I felt devastated that he was leaving. Why did I care at all when he hadn't even factored me into his leaving party? He was probably just going to tell me when he landed in Scotland.

As I turned and leaned back against the door, I saw John standing at the top of the stairs. "There's lasagne in the oven, John, please help yourself." I walked back to the kitchen and switched off the music after telling Dean Martin to fuck off. It wasn't his fault. I then downed the two Aperol Spritzes, as though their very presence was a reminder of my stupidity. After googling whether dogs could eat tomatoes (they can, just not the leaves and stems), I fed the bruschetta to Bingo, who was resting his muzzle on my knee. Then I opened the bottle of ridiculously expensive red wine Madeleine had gifted me and started to get rid of that evidence too. John appeared in the doorway. "That guy is a dickhead." I reached for the remote control and engaged the kitchen blinds. When they were fully shut, he walked in.

"John, join me for a drink."

"I don't drink."

"Why? Are you a bad drunk, are you violent?"

"No, neither of those things."

"Then today you drink," I said, as I poured the remainder of the red wine into the glass I'd assigned for Gomez. He picked it up and stared at it suspiciously, then at me, as though it was poison. I took the glass from his hand, swigged it, then passed it back to him. He walked towards the newly shielded back door, checking it was locked. He came back and stood against the counter.

"John, what is your deal? Are you in trouble with the wrong people? Did you murder someone?" He smiled. He should have smiled more; his brown eyes almost twinkled. As he held his glass, his muscles were bulging from the sleeves of his polo shirt. He had a beard now, and although they really didn't suit most people, somehow, he looked even more attractive. It was a shame he was always so miserable.

"You've spent the last six months thinking I've murdered someone, and in return you offer me lasagne?" I smiled back before he continued, "I guess that explains why you entertain the smug piece of shit that just left."

Great. Everyone knows I'm a fool.

"So seriously, what is your story? Why are you hiding here?" He looked at me without blinking, then briefly screwed up his eyes before searching around the room, like he was looking for a camera.

"You know what, you pick the room, and the next bottle of wine, and we'll go and talk."

He shrugged, picked up his glass and a bottle of Cru Classe Lafite. "Not that one," I said. "That's £3,000." He pointed towards a Bordeaux, and I nodded. He started walking down the corridor, and I followed, guessing maybe we'd go into one of the unused reading rooms, before he started walking upstairs. His room felt the safest, as no one had been in there since he arrived. I walked behind him as he climbed the stairs, transfixed by the definition of his wide shoulders. Every inch of him was so muscular; he was like the Statue of David. I started feeling nervous, being in a bedroom with him, especially with all the times I was alone at night just imagining walking into his room. I had to physically jerk my head to snap myself out of it.

I tried to figure out what it was about him that I found so captivating. He barely spoke, he was always grumpy, he never tried, and he was always rude. Sometimes you try to search for logical reasons, but it's nothing more than nature. Maybe the fact that he didn't say anything was what made it more riveting.

He opened the door and walked in to place his glass and the bottle on the small table in front of the fireplace. I closed the door and walked towards the wooden post of the four-poster bed. He turned to face me and, with a deadpan expression, said, “I should check you’re not wearing a wire.”

I started to chuckle, before realising that his face remained unchanged. “Are you joking?!”

“Nope.”

The one thing I didn’t like about him was that he always looked so intense and serious, but as he started to walk towards me, it was making me wild. Sober me would have just nervously lifted my shirt and quickly flashed my stomach. But drunk me was far more fun. At this point, my evening couldn’t get any worse. I’d just been snubbed by someone I actually did care about, so I wasn’t even bothered if I’d read the situation completely wrong. I started slowly unbuttoning my shirt, trying my best to be seductive. Thank God I was wearing the decent underwear. The whole time, I didn’t drop eye contact. Fuelled by the bottle of wine and two cocktails, I said, “I should probably check that you’re not wearing a wire too.”

Without breaking his stare, he stood and looked at me for a few seconds, considering what to do. I suddenly grew nervous. Had I just made an absolute clown of myself? Then the relief came when, with one arm, he reached behind his back and pulled off his top. He was unbelievably sexy. He had a real man’s body. I’d never seen anything like it. He stayed perfectly still, perfectly quiet, just looking at me, presumably because he wasn’t quite sure what was going on.

After a few seconds, I realised he wasn't going anywhere. I walked over and placed my hands at the top of his trousers and slowly moved my hands over the solid ripples of his stomach. He had so many wounds and scars. One looked like an old bullet injury that had disfigured the top of his chest, which I paused over with my fingers. Out of nowhere, he grabbed my wrist. He didn't like it. He stared at me like he was angry, but then let my arm go and instead cradled my face with his hand and leaned down to kiss me. With his other arm, he picked me up and carried me towards the bed. I had to stop myself from giggling; no one had ever picked me up before, especially not with one arm. I assumed he would be rough or rugged, like Gomez, who was like a pneumatic drill just pumping away. He was strong, gentle, and surprisingly tactile. I'm not sure if it were because the whole thing was so unexpected, because I'd been thinking about it for so long, or because he was just so fucking hot, but I almost passed out with rapture.

Afterwards, I lay there, speechless. Worried that nothing would ever top that moment.

I waited a minute before I said anything. He was lying on his back, looking up, as shocked as I was by what had just happened. It wasn't an awkward situation, but I was worried that I would make it awkward, so then I felt awkward. The first words that left my mouth after the sexiest, most exciting encounter of my life were,

"So, why are you here?"

He laughed. I don't think I'd ever seen him laugh before. I felt my stomach flip, and as soon as he turned and his eyes met mine, I began grinning hysterically.

"Oh yeah, I forgot, an hour ago I was a murderer."

"I guessed if you wanted us dead you would have done it by now." I leaned to face him, softly running my hand over his body as I listened to him talk.

"So, Madeleine never told you? I thought you two were one of the same."

"It's more likely that she was drunk when you spoke to her. She doesn't know why you're here either."

"So, you both live with a stranger, and it takes you four months to speak to me."

"You're not exactly approachable, John. You hole up in your room and… wait, John… that's not your real name, is it?"

He started gently stroking my arm. "Absolutely not."

"You're not going to tell me your real name, are you?"

"Absolutely not," he said again, with that wry, adorable smile.

He took a deep breath and exhaled. "I work for MI5." I laughed. Then I laughed again. Then I saw that he hadn't lost his smile.

"You're not kidding?"

"No." How did that revelation make him ten times sexier?

"That still doesn't explain why you're here?"

"The night you had your Christmas party, when you wore that red sequined dress, I was supposed to go to the safe house next door." I interrupted him by mouthing, 'I fucking knew it,' and he paused, then continued, "Someone I was working with leaked where I was going to some very bad people."

That was quite a lot of intense information, yet my first words were, "At least someone noticed my dress." Followed very quickly with, "Who was it who betrayed you? Are you in danger? Fuck, are we in danger?"

"It's why I clamber around in the shadows. I've spent all my time trying to figure out who it was, and it keeps coming back to the last person I thought it would be. The person I trusted my life with. The one who was family."

Again, the main thing I should have taken from that was that he thought he was deceived by his best friend, and all that was going around my head was the word 'family.'

"I'm not married," he said, as though he'd read my mind.

"So, what now? How will you know?"

"I've left some traps; I have some ways of finding things out. Nothing that could be traced back to here. I wouldn't put you and the mad one in danger. I just needed certain people to think that I was long gone, but I haven't gone rogue. I'm thinking a few more weeks and I'll be out of your hair."
He'd been here for so long, festering in his hole like an angry barn owl, grumbling through the house with his monosyllabic greetings. Thirty minutes of passion and suddenly I'm sad that he's leaving.

"Will we see you again? When you go?"

"Probably not. But I will miss the music."

"Did you really need to check that I was wearing a wire?"

"Only as much as you needed to check that I was," he said with a wicked grin.

The next morning, I opened my eyes to see him sitting up next to me, reading. My hand was lying on his chest still, and I realised that this was probably uncomfortable for him. Gomez would have been able to get up and leave, citing whatever excuse he could think of, but John lived here, and he couldn't go anywhere. I then started worrying that he was waiting for me to wake up so that I would leave. It made me feel uneasy, so I decided to go. I was naked. I didn't have my wine cloak on anymore. I went to pull up the cover and realised there was resistance in the shape of a small springer spaniel. "How long has Bingo been here?" I asked as an icebreaker. "He's slept here every night since he got here. I'm going to miss the little guy." It turns out John had been the one training him, not Mad (which made so much more sense).

"I'm going to head off; I've got a ton of studying to do. I, um, don't suppose you have a towel or a T-shirt?"

"Sure," he said as he got up, wearing nothing but boxer shorts. All I wanted to do was stay in bed with him all day. But I didn't feel the same vibe as last night. He brought over a Judas Priest T-shirt with a smile. "I assume this isn't yours?" I asked as I put it over my head while he got back into bed. "Madeleine brought me a load of her father's clothes. The master suite is still full of things, like someone left in a hurry. What's the deal with that?"

"I think it's quite complicated. Madeleine doesn't like talking about it, and the only other connections to her life are Jude, who is even more defensive than Mad. The other is her friend Lucas, who has probably joined a tribe in Chile by now. I never like to ask. It's a touchy subject."

"Something feels off," he said as he pushed a piece of hair behind my ear. "Just be careful."

I smiled and reached over to stroke his forearm. Then, to my delight, he leaned in to kiss me.

"There's plenty of lasagne, remember," were my last words as I walked out of the room. I wish I could tell you that we made mad, passionate love every night from then on, that I had so much amazing sex that I didn't even have time to care that Gomez had left. But that wasn't the case. I was too much of a wimp to ever approach it again, and John was too much of a gentleman. Or he didn't want me getting attached. Men didn't like to 'lead me on,' apparently. Sometimes maybe it's best to leave something that was perfect and try not to recreate it. A month later, he was gone.

8

The following day, still troubled by John's words and with Madeleine still away, I decided to take the opportunity to explore the other rooms in the house. It felt wrong, almost as though I was betraying her trust by snooping around the property she had so generously allowed me to stay in, no questions asked. Here I was, a stranger in her home, with countless questions. I just had to see for myself, to understand what John meant.

The master bedroom lay in disarray—the bed unmade, laundry still in the basket. Tumblers of water sat on the bedside tables, and on one side was an unlabelled bottle of pills. A small trinket box held a pair of earrings and a wedding ring. The walk-in wardrobe was still filled with men’s and women’s clothes, along with rows of casual and dress shoes. Picture frames sat on the dressing table by the window, containing photographs of Madeleine growing up. Makeup, brushes, jewellery, and hair clips were laid out neatly. I opened two of the large drawers, which were still filled with underwear and hosiery. It was like a ghost ship, mysteriously abandoned. A small closet contained garment bags, scarves, travel bags, and a stack of suitcases. I understood what John meant now—it really seemed as if whoever had left, did so without taking anything. Everything seemed intact, even down to the toothbrushes in the bathroom.

I felt uneasy. If I discussed this with Madeleine, who made it clear she didn't want to talk about it, she'd know I'd gone behind her back, snooping in her house while she was away. I didn't want to jeopardise our friendship; she was the best friend I had ever had. I resolved to try harder to speak to Jude. He seemed to be my only link to her life and her family. How could anyone leave Madeleine by herself? The thought of them abandoning her was heartbreaking. Then I opened the bedside table drawer and almost froze. There were two passports—her mother's and her father's. I sat on the edge of the bed, suddenly realising how little I knew about Madeleine's life beyond the bits and pieces she had shared with me. They didn't even call their own daughter. Just as that thought occurred to me, the landline began to ring, startling me. It was like it had read my mind. I don't know why I thought it might be Madeleine's family, but the timing was uncanny. I picked up the receiver and was met with one of Veruschka's rants. "You know it isn't right, what goes on there." I wasn't sure what compelled me to respond, but when I asked what she meant, she just kept repeating herself. "But what does go on? Why do you keep calling?" I pressed, but all she could say was, "You know why." I didn't know why. I didn't know anything. And that lack of any real explanation—especially since she was speaking to me directly—made the whole situation feel insubstantial. The only thing that troubled me now was the passports.

It was two weeks before Madeleine returned from America. I tried to push the doubts from my mind, but I knew I wouldn't be able to let it go. I wanted desperately to talk to someone about it, but I didn't want to mention it to John in case it caused her trouble. It felt like a betrayal to discuss it with the Chans or Rory &Thomas, as they were her friends. Maybe the lab held clues to the mystery, but it was locked, and I had no idea how to get in. When Madeleine eventually came back, I had her favourite things ready: chilled glasses and champagne. She filled me in on her work stories, her romantic reconciliation with Lucas at Griffith Observatory, and her archaeological dig at La Brea. She paused as she began to open the second bottle and asked, "So, when are you going to talk about what's making you anxious?" I tried the usual response, "I'm fine, what do you mean?"—but clearly, I'm an open book. I wasn't sure how best to tell her that I had completely undermined her trust, hospitality, and generosity by prying through her house in her absence. So, I just let it all spill out.

"Gomez is moving to New York, I slept with John, and I found your parents' passports when I was snooping around their bedroom." Madeleine let the cork pop dramatically, mimicking the sound of an explosion. She was nonresponsive, and I started to panic, fearing I had ruined our friendship. "I'm so sorry I went behind your back. I wasn't even going to say anything until I saw the passports. It really upset me. All their stuff, even their wedding rings, is still there. John told me something felt off, and then Veruschka called, and it's weird that they never try to call you." I could have kept rambling, but I realised I was oversharing with someone who valued privacy. It was a while before she spoke, and her opening words were, "Thank you for your honesty. I would have preferred if you'd come to me rather than investigating on your own." I was tempted to say I'd tried countless times to ask her for information, but it was time to stop talking.

She continued, "My parents have dual citizenship—they have both British and Australian passports. They left their wedding rings because they were in the middle of discussing their divorce. They don't call because I told them not to. Anything else you wish to know?"

There was so much I still wanted to know! Why she was so dismissive and uncaring when they were mentioned. How could they not have tried harder? Why didn't she seem to care? But I realised I'd already pushed things far enough, so I apologised again and took the massive olive branch she offered when she changed the subject to ask for details about my fling with John. I knew she was angry, and in hindsight, it was cowardly of me to pretend everything was fine just to save face. I wonder now if things would have been different if I'd been more honest at the time.

June 14th, 2010

Bingo started barking at the front door, and Madeleine followed him out to meet the postman. It was a rare occurrence—we hardly ever received post or bills. Madeleine claimed she didn't deal with paperwork and assumed someone else sorted it out, but never questioned who or why. I guessed it was her uncle. Madeleine took the ornate envelope and gasped as she removed its contents. "What is it?" I asked, surprising her as I approached. Like Bingo when he'd been caught chewing on something he shouldn't, she tried to stuff it in her mouth. But the stiff buffalo card wouldn't fold, and she began to panic. When I asked her again, she scrunched up her face and reluctantly handed me the invitation. "WHAT THE HELL?" I shouted so loudly that birds fled their nests.

It was an invitation from Gomez's family, inviting Madeleine's family to their son's wedding. "I only saw him four weeks ago. How can you meet someone and propose in four weeks?" It took me a moment to realise it wasn't a four-week whirlwind proposal. "So, what are we thinking? Shotgun wedding or long-term relationship?"

"I don't know," Madeleine whispered sadly.

"Do you know who it is?"

"No, I've never heard her name before."

"I'm such an idiot! I just assumed he didn't want a relationship. I never considered he might already be in one!"

"You're not an idiot. It's never someone's fault if they've been lied to. Why would you ever suspect he was engaged?"

I began angrily drafting a message until I realised he wouldn't care. It turned out that later Madeleine sent him a message of her own, which I found out when he messaged me, saying he "never meant to hurt me" and "never expected things to go as far as they did." He ended with a respectful, "Please don't tell Naomi. She's pregnant, and it would make things difficult for us." When I showed Madeleine, her mouth hung open for so long that a fly flew in, circled around, and then flew out before she spoke.

"That's not an apology!" she finally said. "That's a 'please don't tell my future wife I'm a douche.' He's just guilting you into silence. What did you reply?"

"Nothing. I'm too angry. I'd end up saying something I'd regret. He didn't choose me. I can't shout at him for loving someone else."

"That's not the point! The problem is that he lied to you and to the woman he's marrying!"

"And what do you want me to do? Tell a pregnant woman her fiancé is a cheat? For what purpose? I don't want that kind of drama, and I certainly don't need the guilt."

"So, he just gets away with it?"

"I can't imagine anyone who treats people that way will have a happy ending. They usually get what they deserve."

"And you can just let it go?"

"Honestly, Madeleine, I'm upset. Revenge isn't at the top of my agenda."

"Don't do that."

"Do what?"

"Call me by my name like that when you're angry. It's not my fault he's an arsehole."

"I'm tired. You and I handle things differently, and this isn't helping."

"Fine, let's forget about him and have a day of fun. We can go anywhere; do anything you want."

"I just want to go upstairs, finish my dissertation, and forget all about Gomez and his stupid wife. I hope they have a wonderful life together."

That was the closest Madeleine and I ever came to an argument. We debated almost every evening, but this felt different. I felt judged for being upset, as though I was ridiculous for ignoring her warnings. This, of course, was not the case; these were my own insecurities projected onto her. I was too stubborn to apologise, and Madeleine was too.

Later, there was a light scratching at my door. I thought it was Bingo, but it was Madeleine, holding a priceless bone china serving dish filled with chicken balls from Asia Gardens. She handed them over without saying a word and walked off. I called after her, "Thank you," and she turned and hissed at me. It meant, "I'm still mad at you, but I still love you."

The next couple of years flew by. I spent a lot more time studying, and Madeleine was working on the Hadron Collider project. She joked that the universe could be entirely consumed by a black hole if it went wrong, reassuring me that they also hadn't known if the atomic bomb would end the world—and that had turned out 'alright, all things considered.' I ended up spending more time back in Oxford. Despite her offer of tutoring, Madeleine was rarely around to follow through. I only returned to Devon once during this time, preferring to stay at Gethsemane House even when Madeleine wasn't there. Madeleine and I just had endless fun together; it felt like we lived in our own little bubble. Occasionally, Madeleine would go through her phonebook and invite musicians over to jam in the studio. I never knew where these contacts came from or why they just showed up, but it was the coolest way to spend a weekend. I had the occasional fling, but nothing serious since Gomez. We hadn't spoken in years, not since his message begging me not to tell his wife about us. Before I knew it, I was twenty-four and about to graduate.

Graduation

My parents were unusually dismissive about my graduation, which was strange considering it had been their main focus for years. After three unanswered messages to my mother, I decided to call. That's when she told me that she and my father were getting divorced. When I pressed her for details, all she said was, "You'll have to speak to your father." The tone of her voice made it clear it was bad, and obviously his fault. I blurted out, "Has he had an affair?" The silence that followed for a good ten seconds told me everything I needed to know. "With whom?" I asked. Again, silence.

It turned out my mother had discovered the affair six months earlier but chose not to tell me to avoid disrupting my studies. The worst part was that I'd been home since then and hadn't noticed anything was wrong. But what was worse still was that I wasn't surprised or upset, I almost felt relief. "So, graduation?" I replied. It seemed heartless in retrospect, but Mum had never been one for sympathy. I can only imagine she felt some relief as well. "We'll both be there. We're so proud of you." I had many questions, but it was clear she wasn't ready to talk. I let her go and sat back, reflecting on everything.

I heard a champagne bottle pop in the distance. Mad came outside, holding a bottle of Veuve and two glasses.

"To the second smartest, kindest, and most deserving person on this patio!"

She overfilled both glasses and, noticing my expression, asked, "Why so glum? You got the highest grade possible!"

"My parents… they're getting a divorce."

We both stopped and stared towards the city, bathed in a golden hue, and I tipped back my glass, finishing it in one go. "Shit," said Madeleine, refilling our glasses.

We sat watching the sun go down, talking about anything other than the fresh news. Though I'm usually a good listener, I wasn't much for conversation, and I wasn't sure how I felt. Eventually, seeing that I was struggling, Mad decided to share something about her own parents. We'd been best friends for three years, and although we'd talked about nearly everything, her family was always off-limits.

"I used to love my father. I still don't know why my mother left without saying goodbye. I just remember that when she left, I knew it was his fault. Nothing he did was good. I know you feel your father is the villain right now, but whatever mistakes he's made, you'll find a way to forgive him."

I wish I could say I pushed her to talk more, but I could tell from her expression she didn't want to. We both lay there in silence, respecting each other's pain. Madeleine reached out, held my hand, and we stayed that way, staring forward. Eventually, she jolted up, deciding it was enough. "Oh my God, I forgot to tell you," She shuffled upright, "Veruschka yelled at Rory, saying they've turned her cat gay."

"I'm sorry, what now?"

"Yeah, she completely lost it. She told him she didn't want her cat going into their garden, implied it was unnatural."

"Wow. How exactly does she know her cat is gay? The only unnatural thing on this street is her! She just becomes more unpleasant every time she opens her bigoted mouth. I can't believe I ever took her seriously."

"I asked Thomas how she explained it, and he said we'd have to ask Rory, but he imagined she'd sent the threats with a raven."

Madeleine paused, raising an eyebrow, questioning what I meant by "believing her."

"I mean, I didn't really believe her; she hadn't said anything directly. But she did make me wonder if something wasn't normal."

Madeleine laughed and produced another bottle of champagne. "I'm not sure what normal is, but I can tell you Veruschka is not the one to define it."

"Why didn't you ever tell me you have a sister?" Madeleine rolled her eyes.

"Lucas?"

"Yeah. He said you have a sister in Australia."

"You've waited three years to ask me that! Lizzy, you're an enigma. She's my half-sister, from before Dad met Mum. I've met her a handful of times and never really cared for her. She's insincere, cold, mean and a bully, but my parents love her. The daughter they never had. Anything else you want to know, or can we go back to being miserable?"

"Miserable is fine." I stopped, waited, then continued whining, "You just never share anything with me. I have to learn things from strangers."

"I share my home and life with you. If something's worth mentioning, I'll mention it. Like Veruschka's cat. Everything else is noise."

A murmuration of birds danced in the distance. I raised my glass and said, "Love you." Madeleine smiled, "Love you more."

October 5th, 2013

"I got a message from Gomez yesterday," I told Mad, who frowned in disappointment and put down her coffee. "It's his mum's 60th. He's back in town."

I hadn't heard from him in years. As soon as I saw his name flash up on my phone, my stomach clenched.

"I'm surprised he's in touch. I thought his wife didn't want us talking."

"He's getting a divorce," Mad called out from behind her newspaper, so matter of fact; so blasé. I frowned at her as she peered over the top of the paper. "What was the point of telling you? It wouldn't change anything. He's not moving back."

"It would have been nice to know when you found out, seeing as we live together."

"You're in a good place now! Whenever he's mentioned, you sulk for two days. I didn't see the point. The guy's a waste of space. He didn't want you when he was here, and he doesn't want you now he's divorced. He's less than ten minutes away, and he can't even make time for you before he flies home. Why he messaged you in the first place is beyond me."

"Wow. When does he fly home?"

"Today. Elizabeth, you try so hard to see the best in people that you're blinkered by your own kindness. If I can't tell you the truth, who will?"

"I just think he doesn't want to make it harder by seeing me because his daughter's in Scotland, so he can't move back."

"This is exactly my point! Are you making excuses for him, or are you just trying to make it easier for yourself? Everyone has a villain in their love story, and he's yours."

These sorts of conversations happened with Mad quite often. The only kind of love she understood was tough love, and sometimes her directness was hard to take.

She never knew how to react when I became upset. As tears began to roll down my face, she sighed dramatically, stood up, walked to the fridge, and pulled out some wine. Her way of showing empathy was to make me feel as numb as she did.

"I'm sorry if I sound insensitive. He just makes me so angry."

Without realising it, I picked up my phone to check my messages again.

"Oh my God!" Mad shrieked, watching me.

"Why does he have such a hold over you? Why can't you find a nice guy?"

I found myself questioning why I liked him so much, and the only thing I could think to reply was, "Not everyone wants a nice guy."

We both paused, reflecting on what had just left my mouth.

"That's the stupidest thing you've ever said."

The situation was made worse by the fact that I had no one else to distract me. Over the years, all I'd had were flings. I hadn't met anyone exciting or interesting. Mostly, it was because I lacked the confidence to approach anyone. On the rare occasion I did meet someone, I'd recoil with nerves.

"Mad, I think I'm going to get a job."

"Dear God, why? Do you need cash? Let me give you some money."

"I don't want your money."

"Then why? I thought you were drafting your novel. Aren't we a house of creation? We don't need jobs, like wolves."

"Do wolves have jobs?"

"They must, that's why they're so feral."

"Actually, I do need cash, but not yours. I live here for free, and you're not my partner—we're friends. Imagine if Lucas came back, and you got married. You wouldn't want a third wheel."

"Lucas? What? That's insane! I'd be empty without you! You, Bingo, and mad John—we're a family."

"John left two years ago."

"Really? Gosh, you wouldn't even notice."

"Yeah, I wonder what happened to him. I miss laundry day."

"Wait, so what job would you want?"

"Do you remember when we met Raymond Buckley? He said he could get me a job at *The Inquirer*. He's retiring next year. If I start now and get my foot in the door, it could be mine. I need something that's mine."

"But what about the music and philosophy novel? You were doing so well!"

"Mad, I've written 10,000 words in three years."

"What about the other one? The time travel story we conceptualised. We had the whole plot figured out—the time jumps, the arc, the twists."

"We re-read it the next day when we weren't stoned and realised we'd just written *Back to the Future*."

"No wonder it was good. Lib, I'll support anything you want to do, but whatever it is, don't mention Gomez again. In ten days, we're re-testing the Hadron Collider. It could suck us all into a black hole, and the universe as we know it might cease to exist."

"Do you want to watch *Back to the Future*?"

Madeleine checked her watch. "I don't have to be in Brussels until tomorrow morning. We could probably watch all three if we start now."

10

Raymond Buckley

I met Raymond Buckley when Madeleine and I were playing at Somerset House that summer. It would be our last performance with the current orchestra. Considering the time we'd spent together in rehearsals and performances, you'd think we'd formed strong friendships. You'd be wrong. Everyone was civil with one another, but the group found mine and Mad's friendship odd. They never really tried to get to know us. They'd come to our parties, but only if they were paid, and they'd leave as soon as the final chord was plucked. It was this sort of environment that made making friends so difficult. When the bow finally rolled over the strings for the last note, it was officially over. University was done. The orchestra was done. I was technically jobless and homeless, with no romance prospects and nothing in my diary for the rest of the year.

As we sat back, drinking beer and gazing over the Southbank, it hit me how I'd drifted through the past few years, living only in the moment without considering what was coming. "Stop thinking about it if it's making you upset," was Mad's contribution to my sudden panic. I hadn't considered moving back home, and even the thought was immediately dismissed by Mad's death stare.

Robert came over to talk, and then Raymond Buckley joined us. He was a god. In his early sixties, he was still devilishly handsome. Raymond was a composer and one of the greatest pianists of our time. I stood up to greet him, as though he were royalty. Before I could speak, he held out his hand, praising me for my part in the performance. I couldn't believe my idol was complimenting me. I blurted out, "Please join us," a little louder than necessary and with a hint of desperation.

He did join us, and I listened to him and Robert reminisce while Mad kicked me under the table, urging me to engage. After a few minutes, Madeleine spoke for me.

"Elizabeth is also a composer." Raymond smiled and turned to meet my eyes.

"I'm not surprised. What an absolute talent on the piano. Did you study composition at Oxford?"

"She studied English with philosophy and classical music. She's an even better writer than she is a musician."

I managed to jump in, her mission accomplished. It turned out that not only did Raymond have the musical CV of my dreams, but he also had my dream job. He was paid to write reviews—music and theatre primarily, with the occasional stint as a food critic when the opportunity arose. All over the world. The grandest buildings, the most incredible art, the finest talents. I hadn't even realised someone could be paid to do the things I already did for free.

"I blog about all the performances we see. It's my favourite hobby!"

Raymond then mentioned that he'd only be continuing for another year. If I wanted to send him some of my work, he'd be happy to recommend me for an interview, even if it was just to get my foot in the door until the position became available. Usually, Mad would answer for me, worried I'd be too unsure to take the opportunity. But before she had the chance, I yelled, "YES!" It was the most certain I'd been about anything in years.

Months had passed since that meeting, and I hadn't heard from Raymond. Until last week. After sending him a selection of my reviews and essays, I received no response and assumed he wasn't impressed or that I wasn't a good fit.

"To the contrary," he said. "If I brought you in sooner, they might have pushed me into early retirement. I'll pass your details to the Editor if you're still interested. I'm planning to bow out gracefully after the New Year. Obviously, it's up to them, but I know they'd prefer someone with a musical background—none of which exists in their current pool."

October 15th, 2011

I thought I was still asleep when mariachi music started filtering through my thoughts. The noise grew closer to my bedroom door until it swung open, and Mad came shimmying in with four musicians dressed in bright trajes de charro. Mad was wearing a sombrero and holding two margaritas, which were sloshing all over the carpet due to her incessant wriggling. "HAPPY BIRTHDAY!" she screamed above the music. "It isn't my birthday," I shouted above the bustle. "I know, but in all the time we've been friends, we've never properly celebrated our birthdays!"
"That's because you won't tell me when yours is," I snarled, accepting the tequila-based drink before she lost any more of it. I looked at my phone; it was 6:45 a.m. "Isn't this a bit early?"
"Hold out your hands and close your eyes, and no peeking."
I did what was required of me, as Madeleine jabbed a needle into my arm. "What the fuck was that?!"
"That was Hepatitis A and Typhoid! The vaccination, not the virus. Well, technically it is the virus, but an inactive protein combined with neomycin and..."
"Mad, it's not even 7 a.m. Why the fuck are you giving me vaccinations? This time of day or otherwise, in fact."
"Vacation vaccinations! Vacunas de vacaciones! We're going on holiday! Can you guess where we're going?!"
The look on her face was ridiculous. She could barely keep her eyes in her head. She looked like a child who'd spent the night in a sweet shop.
"I'm going to take a guess and say Mexico."
"YES!!" she screamed.

"I don't even know if my passport is in date," I grumbled, moving my newly vaccinated arm in sore rotations.
Like a magician, Madeleine presented a fresh passport from up her sleeve. I asked her when we were going.
"Now!" she cried, pulling out a suitcase from behind her that she'd somehow packed on my behalf. "Buenos días, mi amigo!"
And so off we went, Madeleine and I, in a private jet from London City Airport to Cancun.

October 31st (Halloween)

The jet lag and aftermath from Mexico meant that neither of us had the energy for a Halloween celebration this year. We decided to invite a few people over to have a scary movie marathon (we were too cowardly to watch horror films by ourselves). I set off on foot to the village to fetch some supplies, namely sweets for any trick-or-treaters (and for us). I bumped into Petra and Dandy outside the Veruschka house, and we laughed about how Halloween must be Abigail's favourite day of the year. Veruschka was hovering over by an azalea bush, pretending to prune it, looking her usual frightening self. Dandy began to bark when a black Mercedes started crawling down Bishops Road. Jude was on his way to see Mad, probably to scold her for daring to take time away from their research to go on holiday. As he approached, it was troubling to see Veruschka's reaction. She looked genuinely fearful, her extremities went limp, and she scurried back towards the house. Movement caught my eye in the top window as her daughter began to retreat and close the curtains. I felt ghosts in my blood. Veruschka was positively timorous at the sight of Jude. She didn't even hang around to deliver her usual taunts, and when I returned from the shops, all the shutters of her house were bolted shut.

Later that evening, in a room full of friends, I mentioned the situation with the Veruschka. Judy Chan immediately shuddered at the mere mention of them. "We should call the police and report that girl being held hostage. She never moves from the attic. She's paler than..." She searched for the right simile—a ghost, milk, snow—and eventually plumped for, "Madeleine." Dan chipped in, "They only leave the house late at night. I don't see anyone else go in or out, and I've never seen them bring in shopping." We reminded Dan that he was stoned most of the time and didn't even realise when his own house was on fire two years ago.

Thomas, who was being unusually quiet, piped up as he was passed a joint and quipped, "I wouldn't be surprised if they both died years ago, and we're seeing their apparitions. That's how creepy they are. Maybe we SHOULD call the police." He searched the room, and we realised he'd accidentally frightened himself instead of us.
Dan replied, "And say what? Hi, a bunch of us got stoned and agreed that our Christian Bulgarian neighbour doesn't fit in, and we don't like that she's different?"
I couldn't help but laugh. "That's not exactly what we're saying. It's more concerns over her daughter."
Dan continued, "We don't know that anything's wrong with her. She may just be an agoraphobe. In any event, I think we should mind our own business. Otherwise, we become just as invasive as Veruschka."

"You can't call the police because your neighbour is a witch," laughed Madeleine, as she rose to her feet and walked towards the door. She came back after a few minutes with four strangers. She clinked her glass with a fork and introduced the crew from Most Haunted. "Ghost Tour!" she shouted. After an hour in the basement, and an hour walking around with night vision goggles, a phasm light, an EVP recorder, an EMF Meter and a sit-down séance with a spirit candle, the Hunters found nothing.

As they led outside, everyone felt both relieved and deflated from the lack of poltergeists. The investigators were loading up the equipment into the van, as Julian found himself drawn to the annexed building that we didn't go in to. He walked over, followed only by the EMF operator, Mad and I. As we approached the lab, Julian froze. "This doesn't feel right," he quivered, as the electromagnetic field monitor began to spike. "It's a lab," assured Madeleine. "There's all sorts of electronic equipment in there that would throw a reading." The assistant holding the EVP recorder noticed a change in frequency, and replayed the recording to his headphones. The colour drained from his face, as he held the earpiece to Julian's ear. They both stared at Madeleine and I like we were abominations. "What happened?" I asked. "What did you hear?"

"Nothing," he replied, before he and the investigator hurried back to their van with speed and unease. I turned to Madeleine, "That was strange." They drove off like they were fleeing a bank robbery.

"Nice ending. They clearly felt bad about their uselessness and wanted to give us a little show. Quite clever really. That was convincing! Now let's go and watch The Ring and watch Thomas cry."

11

The Interview

Two weeks after answering an email, I went to meet the Editor of The Inquisitor, Daphnee Deveraux. Bizarrely, this was my first ever interview, save for the admissions interview for Oxford. Twenty-four years old and no previous employment. "Just lie," said Mad. "Say you worked at the village newspaper for five years. Put Thomas as a reference. They will neither care nor check." But I had my principles, and I didn't fancy starting a new part of my life predicated on a lie. "Then say you were my cleaner. No one will know that the cleaner isn't you."

"Mad, we don't have a cleaner. The cleaner IS me."

"Oh. Really? Well, you're not perjuring yourself then. But if you want a decent reference, you could really do a better job polishing the glassware—the champagne flutes were filthy when I made a Bellini this morning."

I hissed at her, and she hissed back.

"And for some reason, my clothes have smelled musty recently."

"Mad, I'm not actually your housekeeper, and I don't do your dirty laundry. I just clean the rooms we use. The other twenty rooms we don't use are covered in dust."

"Then who washes my clothes?" I shrugged and went upstairs to finish getting ready as Mad stood staring off into the distance, perplexed by her laundry paradox.

The tube station, which everyone told me was a five-minute walk, was a fifteen-minute hike. When I arrived, it turned out I wasn't the only person with this idea. I'd never had to take public transport at rush hour before, and it seemed to reduce people to animals. Every time a train arrived, I politely let the person next to me on first, and after the third train reached capacity and left without me, I realised I was going to have to join in the barbarity. It baffled me how so many people must make the same journey from the same place every day, and yet nobody seemed to know or speak with one another. If anyone accidentally caught the eye of a stranger, they immediately averted their gaze. After twenty-five minutes of cowering under a stranger's armpit, I launched into a commuter's rugby scrum to detrain before surfacing onto the high street.

By the time I navigated to The Inquisitor's headquarters, I only had three minutes to spare. I'd calculated that I'd have a good thirty minutes before the interview to have a coffee, sit, compose myself, and take in my surroundings. As soon as I reached the top floor, I was just about to address the receptionist when a beady-eyed, snake-like gentleman wove his neck around the door and called my name. This was Johnson Jones. Like in most stories, there's always a baddie, and Johnson Jones was my nemesis. A repugnant, small, smarmy, bespectacled little man—planted on earth just to make people as miserable as he was.

He immediately looked me up and down, raising an eyebrow as he did so. He led me through the office as people stopped what they were doing to watch me parade past them as if it were a fashion runway. I forged one of those 'hey' closed-mouth smiles and kept my eyes forward as Johnson opened the meeting room and introduced me to Daphne.

"This is Ellen." He knew my name was Elizabeth; ten seconds prior he'd called my name correctly, but he just wanted to belittle me from the get-go. "It's Elizabeth," I said as I shook Daphne's firm, perfectly manicured hand, maintaining eye contact as Mad had advised me. "You can let go now," she whispered gently. Another piece of Mad's invaluable advice was that during the handshake, I should place my free hand on top of the shaking hands, to show dominance. I chose to ignore this.

Daphne was a stern, confident Black woman in her mid-forties who always commanded a room. She was somewhat of a socialite. Everyone wanted to be her friend, and she was always en route to the most fabulous soirees. Always immaculately dressed and fiercely independent. The kind of woman who didn't suffer fools lightly, yet at the same time, appeared to fall for the charms of Johnson, which always confused me greatly. Saying that, he acted entirely differently around her (like the colour-changing lizard that he was). For all his wickedness, he did his job well, even if he was a repulsively biased and vile human being. I digress. Professional to the core, we never knew much about her personal life, but there were no rings on any fingers and no photographs of family in her office. I felt intimidated by her, but that was my own problem as she was always so nice. You could tell that she had a good heart. Aside from this meeting, I only spoke face-to-face with her one more time, despite seeing her almost every day from then on.

The interview itself was a bit of a disaster. Whenever Daphne and I began to establish a rapport, evil Johnson would butt in and point out a flaw. This flaw was primarily that I had no previous experience. Daphne, whose final decision it was anyway, fought my corner.

The job role itself wasn't yet available, and she decided that due to my inexperience (but mostly sub-editor Johnson's issues with me), if I wanted to, I could start at entry level. It was a touch patronising; I had a degree from Oxford. Johnson followed up with the inference that it was a formality to not 'ruffle any feathers.' They had been down a copy editor since 'Fat Pat' went on maternity leave. It turned out Pat wasn't fat—she was pregnant. But the discrimination lawsuit she filed before departing gave Daphne the impression that she would not be returning.

I would answer directly to the snake. As he showed me back towards the elevator, he told me that I would be emailed a 'zero-hours contract' and I started on Monday. He thumped the elevator button, and his leaving words were, "My friends call me JJ, so you should call me Johnson."

When I eventually made it home, Mad was on a Skype call in the kitchen. She muted herself to ask me how it went. "I didn't get 'the' job, but I got 'a' job… I think?" Then she started to ask me all the questions that I wished I'd asked. Did I have to apply for the role when Raymond left, or would I automatically have the job based on my performance? Was this a trial, and if so, was there an end date to the trial? If the job I wanted wasn't going to be assigned to me immediately, would I have to apply for it, and if so, when? What was the pay, and would the pay increase for the new role? Were any other benefits or expenses included? This list went on. She raised about twenty-five different points, queries, and questions that I should have asked, things that ultimately led to me being walked over. "I've just muted NASA to hear your good news. Can you imagine if I'd forgotten to ask NASA an important fucking question about a space launch?"
"Actually, Madeleine, we're still here," jittered the terrified voice of an older gentleman, to which she slapped the lid of her laptop down to continue shouting at me.
As usual, she was right. The following Monday, I started my first day in my new job.

The New Job

Nothing about this felt pleasant. All the previous excitement had been swallowed up by anxiety. Johnson made it perfectly clear from the moment that I stepped off the elevator that I wasn't welcome. I tried on three occasions throughout the day to ask to speak to him, so that I could address the questions that I so desperately needed to ask. On the third occasion, he shouted (in front of everyone), "YOU ARE ON A TRIAL," and walked off.

There were over a thousand people who worked for the paper; on my floor alone there were about fifty of us. It was incredibly overwhelming, especially when my direct supervisor was the antichrist, and no one showed me what to do. Johnson pointed to an empty cubicle and then slammed a load of files on my desk, together with some digital tapes. "What would you like me to do?" I asked, genuinely bewildered, considering that most of the written files contained hieroglyphics. "Edit the articles on this zip drive, use the notes and the audio, proofread, see if you can make it better." He then rolled his eyes and disappeared for the rest of the afternoon. I really wanted to ask if I had done something to upset him as the hostility seemed highly unnecessary.

I turned on the computer, which had password access. I had no idea how to decipher shorthand and no clue how anything worked. I was on the brink of standing up and just walking home. Then from behind my monitor appeared an angel. Her name was Alison. A beaming, friendly smile, beautifully blow-dried shoulder-length blonde hair, and big kind brown eyes. She couldn't have been much older than me. "Can I help get you settled in? I've asked IT to get you set up on the system—but maybe we can get you a cup of tea and sort out your paperwork?"

I felt like I wanted to cry. A touch of human kindness. Alison was HR, office manager, and Daphne's assistant—the lifeblood of our entire floor. She took me under her wing instantly, and I think without her life would have been unbearable.

"Johnson can be a bit 'tricky,' but he will come around. I get the impression things aren't going well with his wife, and everyone seems to be in the firing line." The truth was, he was just an absolute arsehole. People made excuses for him, but he was torrid.

I met my desk neighbours. Rose, whose job title was feature writer, was like a litter of puppies in a shallow pen, with the nickname 'Wriggly Fidgets.' She was always three coffees in by the time I started, with more energy than a nuclear power station. In the morning meetings, she would always pitch wild ideas for stories but was always shot down and given her pipeline. She was completely celebrity-obsessed and would hustle an invitation to any awards ceremony that brushed shoulders with anyone famous. I could never invite her to any of our parties; she would be a liability. Then there was Adam, a complete geek and computer genius. "He broke up with his girlfriend two years ago because she cheated on him," explained Rose, "and they still live together because she can't afford anywhere else to rent, and he's too kind to throw her out." "And I still sleep on the sofa," added Adam, as he was setting up my login information.
He then asked me if I wanted free Wi-Fi for life. "This place is like 1984, and I am George Orwell." The pure openness of everyone's personal lives was blowing my mind. People were gossiping about people right in front of them, and no one seemed to care. "Be careful what you search for online," whispered Adam as he was still typing. "Johnson asks for a list of everyone's search history at random times. But he doesn't realise that when you delete history, I can still access it, and let's just say I know why he and his wife are having problems." He was to gossip what Madeleine was to science—a savant.

By mid-afternoon, I was still going through the enrolment processes when Johnson came over, asking what I had done all morning. I sheepishly began to explain that I had been having computer tutorials and completing my induction. He didn't say a word. I then made the admission that I couldn't read shorthand as I hadn't done a journalism degree. He went on a massive rant, humiliating me in front of everyone by saying I was useless. I began to feel the adrenaline in my stomach. I wasn't used to someone talking to me like this. I didn't understand why I should sit and take it either.

It was as though people thought the workplace was another dimension, where a job title gave people the right to talk to anyone however they wanted. I was entirely confused how somebody with a mid-level education and intelligence had the right to criticise me about my skills. It was laughable. I was completely shell-shocked that in any situation this was deemed acceptable. We are still living in the real world, are we not? I then heard Mad's voice in my head. "Tell that little weasel to fuck off. Just do it, say 'Fuck off.'"

But this was my first time in the workplace, and I still didn't quite know if this was normal or not. I tried to remain as rational as possible and calmly walked away. This was my first day; whatever grudge he had against me must surely be his bad mood, and tomorrow would be different. Rose told me to just try and be nice to him, but when in any real-world situation would you be nice to somebody who was immediately abrasive and unkind?

I asked Alison later who I would go to if I had any issues. She said, "Johnson." "What if the issue is Johnson?" and she said, "Then you're shit out of luck." By 5 p.m., I was thoroughly exhausted. It took me over an hour to get home, and within an hour of getting back, I was fast asleep.

The next four days were utterly exhausting. Any illusions I had about Johnson becoming more humane were quickly shattered by his appalling behaviour. I did meet some interesting people, though it was so overwhelming that I couldn't take it all in, and only managed to remember a few names. This left me with the awkwardness of asking people their names again because they hadn't made a strong enough impression the first time. I wasn't sure what to make of it yet, mainly because it was simply dreadful being in that environment for 60 percent of my waking hours. I'd spent the last few years meandering around a mansion, playing music, and drinking wine at noon. It made me appreciate getting home all the more. Each evening, I practically sprinted to the tube station, powerwalking down the lane so I could hear Bingo's little claws tinkering on the floor as he raced to greet me.

A few people from the office were heading to The World's End for drinks, which they started talking about at 3 p.m. No one thought to invite me, but that was fine—I just wanted to get out of there.

M was sprawled on the chaise longue in the lounge, drinking with Thomas, while Bingo, George, and Michael wrestled by the fire. Mad raised her glass, "Jesus, Lizbot, where the hell have you been?"

"Work?"

"What, every day?" she asked accusatorily.

"Yeah, it's rubbish. I'm not sure if it's for me. I mean, the job is fine—it's more the atmosphere and the people that aren't. Well, one person in particular."

"Are you talking about the small round-bellied bully? Find out the gossip from the IT guy and send it to everyone in the office. Honestly, Lizzy, I don't understand why you let one person dictate your day."

"Unless it's you?"

"Unless it's me." She handed me a fresh wine glass, and I leaned in to give Thomas a two-cheek air kiss.

"It's not exactly by choice. I know it doesn't sound rational when I say it aloud, but he seems to drain me of all joy. He's a black hole of happiness. I must be imagining that I'm being targeted because it makes no sense."

"Maybe he fancies you?"

"Thomas, he's repulsive, inside, and out. He's been nothing but cruel to me since the moment I met him, and..." I had to stop as I felt a rush of emotion. All the anger I'd bottled up was turning into sadness. Mad noticed my trembling lip and cut in.

"Just quit! You don't need to work at a newspaper to do that job—write your own reviews, freelance for whoever you like."

"You can't freelance without experience, and I don't have any. I need to stick it out for at least a year for credibility."

"You've got a degree with honours from Oxford—that's your credibility." Bingo nuzzled up to me, and stroking his happy little face began to soothe me. I understood what M was saying, but leaving felt like admitting defeat, as though I was letting Johnson win. If only I could go back and tell myself that I should have trusted my instincts. Negativity like his spreads like cancer, and the only way to stop it is to cut it out.

I decided to spend the weekend working on all the long-term articles that needed editing, so I could walk in on Monday ahead of the game. I set up my laptop in the orangery and watched the gardeners patch up the holes Bingo had dug and wrap the plants to protect them from frost. Mad was heading to Florida for work the following week, leaving me in charge of Bingo and the house. After I took the job, Mad started going away more often, feeling there was less point in being around when I wasn't.

The good news was that everything I'd edited was well received. Johnson almost winced as he begrudgingly admitted that I wasn't "completely useless" (his words). Buoyed by this, I asked him if we could have a quiet word. He dismissed me with, "I'm busy. Keep trying, and we'll be fine." He couldn't even pretend to be decent. He wasn't busy—he went back to his desk, and I could see the reflection of his solitaire game in his Penfold glasses.

What baffled me was how robotic everyone was. No one seemed to be themselves. When we finally went for the first round of work drinks, almost everyone was different. Was it that people believed they had to act a certain way to be "professional"? If everyone knew this and felt this way, why didn't anyone do anything about it? It was no different to the strict rules of prison. From school, you're taught to conform and respect people who give you no reason to. Just their position—which, let's be honest, some people weren't even good at. They used it to exert some imagined power, desperately trying to feel important.

"The only difference is that, unlike prison, you could leave," agreed Rose. But you were mentally imprisoned, conditioned to stay for the money and convenience. Finding new jobs required effort, and when did you have the time? You were always exhausted from work, unable to dip out for interviews. Then there was the uncertainty—what if you didn't get the job or it was worse? Better the devil you know, right? And let's not forget that you'd lost all confidence by this point. There was the fear people would talk, the horror of your current employer finding out you were trying to leave, making everything worse. That's why I stuck around. Every day, enduring Johnson's nonsense demands and listening to the shallow ramblings of the uninspired, hoping that eventually it would all pay off.

12

Fast-forward three weeks.

Mad's welcome-home party on Saturday, which consisted of just us, Rory, Thomas, and the Chans, carried on through to Sunday, making Monday morning even more dismal. I hadn't had the courage to wash my hair, and it stank of tequila and cigarettes as I stood on the tube. To my and my fellow commuters' revulsion, I sprayed it with the ancient bottle of perfume in my handbag, and we all choked in our confined huddle. I was later than usual. The queue for coffee was insane, but I couldn't face arriving without caffeine. Weighing up the consequences, I concluded that you can't be late twice. I dashed into the morning meeting, where everyone sat fresh-faced, hanging on Daphne's every word.

After apologising, I slunk into the nearest chair, keeping my head down. In doing so, I didn't notice the tall blonde woman at the top left of the table next to Johnson. As Daphne handed the meeting over to him, Johnson walked to the front looking disgustingly smug. He addressed me with a chilling smile before beginning, "Glad you all could make it." I wondered why he was so pleased with himself. When he announced Evelyn Winters as the new candidate for the role I'd been working towards for six months, I knew why.

She stood up and stretched out her arms, gently covering his wrists before shaking both his hands. From a distance, she seemed strikingly beautiful, though imperfections became apparent as you drew closer. Her long, perfectly curled blonde hair flowed effortlessly atop her £2,000 suit. Her lips were garishly large; she'd had implants in her cheeks and, presumably, Botox in her unusually broad forehead. She had false eyelashes and wore more eye makeup than I did for the school production of *Grease*. She looked about thirty, though I later realised she was younger—just twenty-five. She began speaking in a well-spoken American accent.

"Now, I know a lot of you think I'm a nepotism baby, but I promise you the same thing I promised my father: I will work my ass off at this job…"

I met Alison's eyes and glared at her in disbelief. She was gently shaking her head.

"I don't know much about your history or culture, but I'm going to give it my all! Go Team *Inquirer*."

She didn't even know the name of her father's company.

Alison pulled me aside afterwards to fill me in. Evelyn was the daughter of the US founder's great-great-grandson. She'd studied drama at Juilliard, and that, apparently, qualified her for the role. She hadn't even taken English past high school, and judging by her size-zero waist, she didn't eat either. Johnson met her at the New York Christmas party and began pushing for her to join the UK office to take the role Raymond was vacating. When I'd shown up under his recommendation, I'd potentially scuppered his plans to work with the elegant Evelyn. Imagine his delight when he convinced Daphne that I was an excellent copy editor and that it was the role I was born to fill.

Daphne, far too principled to be strong-armed into hiring someone based on family connections, would never have agreed unless it benefitted the paper. Johnson spent the last 20 weeks persuading her that my talents were better used tidying up other people's work, never showing her anything I'd submitted separately.

I left the meeting room feeling utterly defeated.

I told Alison I was taking the day off. Why did unwelcome news always come with a hangover? Johnson, overhearing and knowing I was integral in showing Evelyn the ropes, tried to intervene, saying I couldn't leave without a doctor's note.

I looked at her, then at him. "She's going home," said Alison, nodding at me. I walked out of the office and stayed home for the rest of the week, unsure if I'd return.

It's strange, isn't it, how sometimes you just know? I didn't know anything about Evelyn—I hadn't even heard of her before today. Yet something in my bones told me that no matter how hard I tried, I wasn't going to get that job. Madeleine told me if I wanted to manifest it, I had to change my mindset, but no amount of affirmations would get in Johnson Jones's way. It was the same instinct that told me Gomez would never change, though I remained hopeful that one day things would be different.

It's also strange how you think about someone, and it's almost always when you look your worst, that you bump into them. There I was, walking away from the *Inquirer* headquarters, on the phone to Mad, already emotionally raw from the weekend and on the verge of tears, when none other than Gomez started walking towards me. I hadn't seen him in almost three years, and of course, it had to be today. "Oh no. It's Gomez."

"Elizabeth, NO!" Mad cried as I slapped the phone shut.

"Dad, I've got to go—I've just bumped into Morticia Addams. I'll call you back." He put the phone in his pocket and opened his arms for a hug. "My fictional wife!" he bellowed cheerfully. I needed to get out of this situation. I wanted to find an open manhole and jump in it.

"I didn't know you were back in the UK?"

"Yeah, I've been back for a few weeks, just catching up with family and friends."

A few weeks. Everything about this day was becoming increasingly insulting. I still didn't fall into the "friends" category.

I began telling him about my exciting new job and how everything was going brilliantly—all lies. I wanted to cry. I wanted to tell him how much seeing him had ruined an already awful day, how I'd spent three years wondering what our lives could have been like if he'd just stayed. But what was the point? When he commented that my power suit was hot, my already shattered self-esteem took the bait. I was such a sucker. He asked where I was heading, and when I said home, he asked if I wanted to share a cab back. Instincts kicked in again, so I asked if he was actually separated from his wife.

"We're trying to make it work for our daughter, but we haven't had sex for six months if that's what you're asking. It's not going to work out."

I couldn't believe what I was hearing. For the first time, I was genuinely shocked. Had he always been like this, and I was just too infatuated to notice? Either way, I said it was nice to see him and walked away. What I wanted to do was call him out on his vile behaviour. "No, I wasn't asking about your sex life. I was checking to see if you were still an arsehole, which you are!" I was furious.

I was about to call M back—but not immediately, as I was choking up, tears streaming down my face. I wanted somewhere to sit down until it passed, but there wasn't a bench in sight. I began walking back to Madeleine's. By the time I reached Archway station, I noticed a car creeping alongside me, the sound of an electric window lowering, and Samuel Barber gently drifting through the wind. It was the song I'd told M I wanted at my funeral. "It's okay, Elizabeth, you didn't die today," M soothed as she pulled up in her F-Type Jaguar. "Get in the car, you silly bitch—you're in no state to walk."

Bingo's beautiful little nose was poking out the window, and the sun appeared from behind the clouds. I couldn't help but smile. Why did I seek validation and happiness from people I didn't even respect? I'd forgotten what was truly important, and I was annoyed that it had affected me so much. I'd been so sheltered in Madeleine's mansion, surrounded by beauty and friendship, that I wasn't prepared for the ugliness outside those walls.

Alison called me, away from prying ears and recorded phone lines. "I really don't think you need to take this too seriously. Evelyn will last a month, maybe two, with Johnson's help. It was agreed in the staffing meeting that you'd be promoted to Copy Editor, with a nice pay rise—up to £45k a year, which Daphne pushed for. I guarantee, as soon as she realises what an absolute potato sack Evelyn is, she'll be out the door. You just need to hang in there."

"Can you put the rest of the week down as annual leave? I hear what you're saying, and it makes sense. I just need a rest. I feel exhausted."

"I'll do whatever you need. But as a friend, I wouldn't recommend more than that. Johnson really is a special kind of piece of shit. Don't jeopardise your future because of him—you're too talented."

I hung up and paused for a moment. "M, fancy getting out of town for a few days?" She indicated and turned the car around by Highgate hospital. "You bet your arse we can. Where shall we go?"

"Just drive. Head south. Let's find the seaside." On cue, Bingo started wagging his tail, as though he knew we were off to the beach.

Calais

"When I said south and the beach, I didn't mean France," I laughed as we joined the queue for the Channel Tunnel.

"I don't even know if Bingo speaks French."

An hour and a half later, we landed in Calais. Within 30 minutes, we were sitting outside a café with a cheese board and a bottle of red wine, having bought a pair of sunglasses and sunhats from a nearby souvenir shop. We had no luggage, no plan, and nowhere to stay. Classic Madeleine. It was there that the idea to finish the VR project was born. She had been working on an interactive gaming headset with Jude for years—a project he and her father had started. She began one of her rants about the future of technology. Artificial intelligence was going to change the world. With a slip of the tongue, she began explaining the cognitive processes involved in bypassing headsets and the capabilities of the human brain. "Intuitive attunement and receptive access each have a particular phenomenology. We have a conscious contemplation of unconscious resources. My father had been saying it for years," she said, stopping herself, suddenly embarrassed to have mentioned him so enthusiastically. She went to do her usual thing, withdrawing into herself, so I kept asking questions to maintain her momentum.

"But how can you convincingly go to places you've never been before?"

"Have you ever been to Calais before today?"

"Nope."

"But would you say it's lived up to your expectations? Is it how you imagined?"

"Pretty much, yeah."

"Your brain collects and stores so much data, and you'll only access 1% of it in your lifetime. Think about how many films you've watched. You could go anywhere you've ever wanted and recreate it through unconscious thought. Even if you haven't heard or seen enough to visualise it fully, your imagination is powerful enough to piece it together."

Mad went quiet again. She took a sip of her wine and began doodling on a napkin.

"I'm going to do it. I'm going to finish what my father and Jude started."

"What did they start?"

"A neuromorphic chip that will change the way we understand the human brain."

I raised my glass to the air. "And I'm going to finish my book of rat drawings."

Monday Morning

Upon returning to the office after our trip to France, I felt a growing sense of anxiety throughout the journey in. Before I even had the chance to put down my bag and set my coffee on my desk, Johnson clicked his fingers at me like I was a dog and beckoned me into the meeting room.

"I need you to start showing up. Disappearing when we needed you to help Evelyn with her induction was unacceptable. I had to fight to save your position and secure your promotion."

This wasn't true, and I couldn't even hide the smirk forming on my face. "Is something funny?" he snapped. There was nothing funny about it. It was the least humorous experience I'd had in years. I recalled Alison's words and decided it was best to just play along.

"Johnson, I'm not sure what you mean by induction. Surely Ray Buckley would handle the handover? He's the one whose position she's replacing. I'm just a copy editor."

"You're so clever, aren't you, Leslie, with your Oxford wit." He still never called me by my actual name, as though it was some kind of psychological warfare, a way to break me with his ignorance. "Your job is to edit her work, amend it, adapt it—do what you're paid to do. Remember, her father is Daphne's boss. You could try a little harder around here and show some respect to your superiors."

"Kleiner Wixxer," I muttered under my breath.

"Sorry?"

"I said that's fine," I replied, standing to leave.

The only thing he was superior to was the Bubonic Plague.

August 2012

Two months had passed since Evelyn (known to us as "Evil Incarnate") joined the office. If you're wondering what kind of person she was, she was exactly the kind of person Johnson adored and who exploited that adoration to her advantage. She was manipulative, spiteful, underhanded, and passive-aggressive. Yet, she wasn't entirely stupid—she knew how to twist situations to her benefit. What she lacked in education, she made up for in cunning.

The daily barbs and digs were slowly eroding me, and I barely noticed I was becoming numb. I didn't even fight back. It started with the bullying: pointing out if I was late in front of the whole office or reading my personal emails aloud to everyone if she caught me writing them. When I came in hungover (which became more frequent after she started), she made sure everyone knew, reminding them throughout the day. Comments on my clothes, my makeup, backhanded "compliments" like, 'You look so much better when you make an effort.'

She was one of those people so full of hate that it felt pointless to defend yourself unless you had the energy, which I surely did not. Especially not when her ally was my second least favourite person in the office—or the universe. At first, I would just zone her out, internally monologuing with thoughts like, 'You absolute, useless parasite. I hate you.' Then she'd finish talking, and I wouldn't have heard a word she said. I stopped even trying to hate her. I just blocked her out and interacted only when necessary. If you're wondering if she was good at her job, her work was even more inexcusable than her behaviour.

"Take it to Daphne," Alison said after I showed her a printout of Evelyn's review of *Cats*. "There's no way Daphne won't read that and see she's a joke, no matter who her father is."

"Johnson told me it was my job to take her work and edit it. I told him it looked like a child wrote it, and he said if I didn't want to do my job, he'd find someone who would."

"What are you going to do?"

"I'm thinking of tidying up the grammar and just submitting it. I wrote a better review of *Cats* on my blog when I was twelve—they'll know it wasn't me."

I executed my plan. The published review received positive feedback—Johnson had re-written it. I started compiling Evelyn's raw drafts in a folder, alongside my own work. When the time was right, I'd sit down with Daphne and make my case.

13

Hawaiian Party

Mad and I were in the studio with Mick the bassist and Stephen Cassidy, messing around recording songs. We were trying to immortalise our drunken idea of a classical hip-hop album, *Philharmonic Beats*. Mad got increasingly animated, spiralling into a passionate rant about how we were going to revolutionise music with this unique fusion. She started playing a load of hip-hop tracks, pointing out where we could layer over orchestral arrangements. I was feeling relaxed after some potent weed, which seemed to have no effect on Mad, who busied herself creating our new band. She registered websites, ordered merchandise, sent emails to her contacts, and posted ads for auditions. When we checked her handiwork the next morning, we discovered she'd accidentally ordered two hundred T-shirts. Thanks to an unfortunate autocorrect, they all said, "Philharmonic Breasts." She took this as serendipitous—I did not and refused to be in the band.

Mad fanned herself with sheet music and declared, "I need an iced drink. We should have a Hawaiian party tomorrow night."

"I'm not sure how those two statements are connected. Isn't it a bit short notice?"

"Only if you lack imagination," she retorted, playing the opening chords of Beethoven's *Symphony No. 5*.

As usual, whatever she planned somehow materialised to a standard that would take most people months to organise. Everyone gathered, enjoying the unusually glorious weather, dressed in garlands, coconut shell bras, and hideous Hawaiian shirts. I found a hibiscus flower dress at the market, complete with a matching plastic flower for my hair. I found Mad in the kitchen, filling large jars with Piña Colada mix, wearing a tight black mini dress and vintage Gucci sunglasses.

"You don't look very Hawaiian," I said through gritted teeth, feeling ridiculous in my garish neon blue and pink smock.

"Well, this is what I wore when I went to Hawaii."

The Hawaiian night was in full swing. Madeleine had reluctantly agreed that I could invite Alison, on the basis that she had been kind to me. I joked that she was jealous, to which she responded by putting an apple in her mouth, mimicking the hog roast next to her. What I didn't expect was how well she and Alison would get along. After two hours of watching them giggling, I started to think Madeleine was doing it as an example, but it was genuine. And, it turned out, I was the jealous one. I stood next to Rory, who asked me who Mad's new best friend was, before placing a lei around my neck and quipping, "First lei you've had in ages." Sadly, he was right.

September 2012

Mad was completely engrossed in her project and had flown to the US to collaborate with her uncle's team at MIT. She had helped them with their battery-powered car, and in return, got access to his tech team's expertise. The house was quiet and eerie. My life had become a monotonous routine of work and solitude. Every morning, I would wake up to Mad's alarm instead of setting one an hour earlier for myself.

I would have a bath the night before to save time, so all I needed was some perfume, body lotion, and a toothbrush. I used to try with my appearance, but now it was basic: foundation, blusher, a lick of mascara, and a bit of eyebrow pencil to compensate for my overplucked eyebrows of the '90s.

I power-walked to the tube station, usually around the same time that Petra Zimmer walked her golden retriever. I always stopped to pet Dandy; they moved at the same leisurely pace. No matter what time I arrived at the tube, it was always packed to the rafters. Ten minutes of hovering amidst strangers, and I'd follow the crowd across the road to the coffee shop. Despite taking this journey almost every day for nine months, I don't think I'd seen the same person twice. Surely, that couldn't be true. I'd order a sugar-free vanilla latte, sometimes a pain au chocolat if I were hungover, and then walk the 10-12 minutes to work in time for the 9 am morning meeting. Evelyn would inform everyone she had come from Chelsea and still managed to get here by 8:45 am, having had breakfast and been to the gym. This never grew tiresome for her.

I'd check my morning emails, read the headlines, and note any upcoming events or print deadlines to prioritise. I'd start reading an article, correcting grammar, and spelling as I went, then read it again, and once more to rewrite it until it was a decent piece. At midday, I'd put my headphones in and walk down to the sandwich place on the corner, dawdle around the shops, then sit in the park to eat. On Fridays, Alison and I sometimes went to eat by the Lock or wandered around the market looking for interesting street food. Occasionally, some of us would go for a boozy lunch, and if we thought we could get away with it, we wouldn't go back to work—especially if we knew Johnson was out.

The afternoon dragged, and I'd often finish everything by 3 pm. I'd then browse the internet for upcoming shows, restaurant openings, or concerts to try and persuade Mad to attend.

I'd catch the tube home at 5 pm, get out of the work clothes, and into something comfortable. I barely bothered cooking anymore. Even when Mad was home, she didn't eat. I'd just make something on toast—beans, soup, eggs, jam, cheese—whatever I could find. I'd watch *The Simpsons* at 6 pm, then take a bath while listening to Chopin.

I could be drafting the book I've been trying to finish for the last five years. When I say "finish," I use the term loosely, as only 15,000 rough words exist. If I put as much effort into writing it as I did into making excuses not to, I'd be on my third bestseller by now. Even though I was doing nothing but pottering, drying my hair, painting my nails, making tea, I seldom made it to sleep before midnight. Then my mind would start to race, thinking of all the things I wanted to do, all the things I'd like to say, all the risks I wished I could take, all the people I could tell to get bent. Despite doing nothing, it still seemed to consume all my time.

The morning of the 7th of September was no different, apart from the laundry I'd been putting off for weeks finally catching up with me. You know it's bad when the only knickers left are bikini bottoms, and the only bra has an underwire that digs into your underarm by midday. You always try to tuck it back in, hoping it will behave, because you can't bring yourself to throw away your favourite bra. Every usable piece of workwear was crumpled in a basket, buried under a week's worth of old clothes. I managed to cobble together an outfit—an old beige corduroy skirt, a navy cardigan with embroidered gold cats, and a black silk shirt underneath. It wasn't ideal; I looked like I'd lost a bet and had to wear clothes bought entirely from a charity shop. If it weren't for the damp towel on top of that laundry mire, I might have salvaged something with body spray.

I wore bright red lipstick, thinking it would distract from my outfit. I'd go shopping at lunch, so if I were too worn out later, I wouldn't need to face chores again. The day began as usual—a rushed commute, a packed tube, a pain au chocolat since I was four minutes ahead of schedule. I walked into the morning meeting, oblivious to the confused looks I received, having already forgotten about my eclectic outfit. I was equally unaware that I had lipstick on my teeth and chocolate smudged around my mouth.

Rose was overly enthusiastic about the cat cardigan, telling me about all the cats she'd seen on her way to work. She was a bit bonkers. Evelyn didn't like seeing me smile. She crumpled her face in an attempted frown, though with her Botox, it was hard to tell. "Interesting outfit," she commented from across the room.

"Thanks," I replied, mirroring her squinty stare.

"It wasn't a compliment," she sneered, looking at Johnson. They both laughed like a pair of rabid hyenas. Alison caught my eye and subtly rubbed her tooth, pointing out the lipstick. Thank goodness for sweet Alison.

The clatter of kitten heels echoed from outside the room, and although my back was to the window, I knew it was Daphne. As if in unison, the five women sitting opposite me bore shocked expressions, mouths agape as if the President of the United States had walked in. Was Daphne having a wardrobe crisis too? I turned to look, expecting to see her in a similarly bizarre outfit, and instead adopted their expressions. Alongside Daphne was the most perfectly handsome man I'd ever seen. Everyone immediately sat up, straightening their posture weakened by the drudgery of office life.

'What a day to choose to dress like an absolute lunatic,' I thought. Evelyn was immediately all over him, tossing her hair so often it could cause a vortex. He stood at the front of the room, delivering some corporate spiel. I got lost in it, studying his mannerisms, the confidence of his smile. He was almost too perfect. When someone is that attractive, you know they know it.

I found myself grimacing at his clichéd, inspirational words. It was all very rehearsed, but when he scanned the room and caught my eye, I had to look away to hide a smile. Revolting. I felt dirty and disgusted for finding him so appealing. I bet he would describe himself as charming. I hadn't felt this flustered since Gomez. I was so distracted; I didn't even realise when he announced he was joining our office. I only realised when everyone started clapping.

"This may seem a tad cheesy," he began, "but I always find a good icebreaker is if everyone stands and says their name and an interesting fact about themselves." I almost gagged. How could someone that good-looking be so annoying? Everyone was eager to introduce themselves. Lisa Symons visibly unbuttoned her shirt before her turn, and Rose began tightening her bra straps. Evelyn stood to announce she was runner-up for Miss New York last year, giving him a coy wink as she sat back down. I was next. I hated this sort of thing and started to feel anxious—not because I had to speak, but because I suddenly realised I had nothing interesting to say. I felt painfully dull. Why hadn't I finished my book? At least then I would have accomplished something.

Before I could say anything, Evelyn mimicked in a baby voice, "I once played piano at the Royal Albert Hall." She was such a jerk. I smiled, turned to her, then looked back at New Guy and said, "Yes, that. And my name is Elizabeth."

The fact that her taunting had now escalated to group mockery didn't surprise me, nor did Johnson's participation in her raucous laughter. New Guy, clearly taken aback by her behaviour, said in a politician-like voice, "That's incredibly impressive. No wonder people are jealous."

Okay, maybe I was too quick to judge.

After the meeting, I was waiting for the kettle to boil in the canteen when Alison bounded in, demanding to know why I didn't defend myself.

"Why didn't you say something?!"

"Because I despise her. I don't want to become her."

"But by not saying anything, you let her win!"

"That's not true. She can't even win Miss New York," I quipped, realising we weren't alone when New Guy spat out his coffee laughing.

"Good one," he managed, taking another sip. He turned to leave and winked as he did so. Who winks? My new crush, that's who. Mine and every other person in the office/building/borough/country. I felt ridiculous on the tube ride home, covered in bags of new clothes. Next time Evelyn humiliated me, I would at least look good.

14

12th September 2012

I was particularly incensed today when Evelyn's "work" was not only appalling but offensive. I usually didn't bother taking anything to Johnson anymore, as he was too enthralled by her, but even he, as a journalist, should have found this unacceptable. He leaned back, looking at what she had written.

"You've seen the play?" he asked. I nodded, stupidly, unable to lie. "You'll be able to straighten this out then."

"It says 'The Book of Joseph, by Harman/Hollander/God!'"

Johnson shrugged.

"It has nothing to do with God! It's about a Jewish family's correspondence during Nazi-occupied Poland, and she's talking about Jesus being sold as a slave! She's googled 'Book of Joseph' because she couldn't be bothered to see the play, and she's probably never read a book in her life! She concludes by saying, 'Every day lasts a year, which is probably how God made the world in seven days.'"

I waited for a response, a reaction—anything. He glanced at the offending paragraph and didn't even flinch.

"You don't find it distasteful that she's mistaken the resilience of a family surviving genocide for some garbled nonsense about the Egyptians?"

"Eliza, she made a mistake. It's easily done. I'm sure you can correct it accordingly." He screwed up the paper and tossed it in the bin before dismissing me with a wave.

"Schiesskopf," I muttered as I left.

September 14th, 2012

Mad kept nagging me to take a photo of New Guy, and after a week without one, she threatened to come to work to see him for herself. Knowing she wasn't bluffing; I tried to sneakily hold up my phone and pretend I was texting. No one was looking, so I snapped the photo—completely forgetting that the flash was on. My stomach dropped, and I almost threw up right there at my desk. New Guy instantly looked up, both seeing and hearing the flash, and there was no doubt it was directed at him. I stared at my phone, acting as if it had gone weird, turning it around, tapping it on the table as if it were broken. I immediately emailed Alison. She must have seen I was typing because she pre-empted me with her own email: "No, you can't go home."

When I finally looked at the photo, there was New Guy, staring straight at me, his eyes reflecting the flash like giant yellow headlights. Safe to say, I laid low for the next few weeks. Evelyn started going around taking close-up photos of everyone with the flash on, saying, "My bad, my phone's broken," and then turning to look at me and laugh.

September 17th, 2012

I walked into the office foyer with a coffee in one hand and my phone in the other, trying to reply to Mad's message. She was rambling about inviting 'Most Haunted' to the house again to see if we could do a Ouija board in the lab. As the elevator door opened, I suddenly felt someone's presence beside me. I looked to my left, and there he was—New Guy. He was so handsome it made me shiver. We both said "morning" and then stood silently as we began our ascent. Every second of silence felt like an hour, and I nervously filled the void by blurting out anything to avoid the quiet. I could have asked how he was settling into his new job, if he liked London, or even if he liked the UK. But instead, I said, "What would you rather see, a ghost or an alien?" He raised an eyebrow in surprise but seemed to consider his answer.

"I think it would be a ghost," he said, "because I feel that aliens must exist somewhere in the vastness of the universe." Instead of just nodding and accepting his answer, I decided to be contrary and said, "My best friend is an astrophysicist, and she debunks the theories of similar advanced life elsewhere." He nodded as we reached our floor, leaving the lift looking confused. But not as confused as I was. What on earth was I thinking?

Two days later, we met again in the lift, this time joined by some people from the third floor. When they got off, leaving just the two of us, he turned to me and said, "Alright, what would you rather: time travel four times, or teleport forever?" You could have knocked me over with a feather.

"Can I take anyone with me?" As soon as I said it, it sounded like I was asking him to traverse time and space with me. He thought about it for a moment. "No, just you."

"Hmm, then I'd say time travel. It would be disappointing to teleport anywhere in the world but not be able to share it. I'd love to meet my grandad and see my grandma when she was my age. What about you?"

"I mean, it would be mighty tempting to pop to Italy for pizza whenever you wanted." I imagined us sitting in Italy, outside a trattoria, eating pizza and drinking a cold glass of Chablis in the evening sun. He looked at me like he could read my thoughts. He continued, "But I'd give anything to go back and spend more time with my mum before she got sick." He looked genuinely choked up, and it formed knots in my stomach. "I'm sorry," I quivered as the doors opened. He cleared his throat and stepped out, saying, "Your turn next."

This became our little game. When it was just the two of us, we'd play our fun little game. Our other interactions were strictly professional. I didn't think it was possible to fall for someone over a game of 'Would You Rather' in a lift, but apparently, it was.

September 22nd, 2012

The office was sweltering. We were having an extended summer, and it was a balmy twenty-four degrees, yet for some reason, the heating in the office was on full blast. The reason was Karen Porter. That woman could sit in an active volcano and still shiver. She had no flesh on her bones, no circulation either, yet she wore only a flimsy shirt year-round. Everyone in the office had beads of sweat rolling down their foreheads, and the moment anyone tried to open a window, she'd leap out of nowhere like a feral cat to slam it shut. Some of the over-fifty-fives were concerned they had catapulted into early menopause until they realised Karen controlled the thermostat. A few of us decided enough was enough, and we were going to switch the heating to air conditioning—until we noticed New Guy taking off his jumper, revealing a tight black t-shirt. We decided Karen could keep her heat.

September 25th, 2012

I've found myself trying to be at work on time so I could run into New Guy in the lift. I considered loitering in the lobby, but then realised that was basically stalking. If we bumped into each other, it had to be organic. Today was my lucky day; he was waiting in the foyer on a call when I arrived. I waved good morning, shuffled past, and called the lift as he held up a finger and mouthed, "One sec," finishing his call.

"Alright," he said as we stepped into our carriage. "Would you rather spend a year in prison or two years in a coma?"

"That's too easy. Prison. I could focus on chin-ups, press-ups, and reading books in bed all day. The alternative is that your muscles would atrophy in a coma, your throat would be ruined by intubation, and you'd be pale as a ghost. What about you?"

"Coma for me. Prison is different for a man."

"I get that. Alright, my turn. Would you rather live in a treehouse with no internet or an underground bunker with no daylight?"

"Can I use the internet at work?"

"Sure, but only for work purposes. The all-seeing Adam would be monitoring your search history."

"I'd expect nothing less. Then the treehouse. You?"

"No contest—treehouse. I'd feel too claustrophobic in the bunker. I need daylight." We reached our floor, and, as usual, the time went too quickly.

October 9th, 2012

It had been nearly a month since New Guy started. Evelyn had no reason to talk to him, yet she was always in, on, or circling his office like a vulture whenever she could. Spanish Marcus, who sat two desks away from me, was convinced she wasn't even interested in him; she was only doing it because she knew I liked him.

He was the only Marcus in the office, but for some reason, everyone prefixed his name with "Spanish" because he went to Barcelona once.

Mad was back from her conference in Copenhagen and had brought a magician back with her to stay until our Halloween party. She forwarded me a copy of the invite, which I then forwarded to Alison at her request. Since Gomez was no longer a friend, Mad decided to design this year's invites herself. They were... well, less elegant than previous efforts. It looked like a child had used a Photoshop template, complete with a Hammer Horror-style font that read, "Hold onto your knick-knacks, fuckers—it's Halloweenus!" above a cartoon penis with a vampire cape. I made a mental note to speak to her before she took it upon herself to do the Christmas invites too.

Suddenly, the office pinged in unison as fifty email alerts went off at once. I looked at the notification on my screen. It was an email from me—to everyone. I'd sent it to "All" instead of just "Ali." This wasn't just limited to the fifty people on our floor; it included the entire building. I'd just invited the whole office—including New Guy, Johnson, and Evelyn—to my party.

I looked over at Daphne, who raised her eyebrows so high I could see the whites above her pupils. I'd sent a Dracula penis invite to the Editor-in-Chief. She pondered her response, looked up at me, then back at her keyboard, before slamming her laptop shut and heading out to lunch. She said nothing. I pushed back on my chair and headed past Alison, pointing towards the kitchen.

"What the hell just happened?" she asked, her eyes alight with mischief, trying hard to be sympathetic but finding it difficult not to laugh.

"I just sent Count Dickula to my boss and the rest of the company, that's what happened."

"Why?"

"It wasn't on purpose! It was meant to be just for you, but it went to everyone. What do I do?"

"You could try recalling the email, but I think everyone has already read it."

"Should I send another email saying it was a mistake, and no one is invited, or say they're invited but the invite was a mistake? Which is worse?"

"Depends. Do you want everyone to come?"

"Of course I bloody don't! But I also don't want to look like an idiot." (Alison raised an eyebrow.) "Okay, even more of an idiot. Damn, I feel physically sick."

"Well, you can't go home. I'd just leave it. I doubt anyone will come—you know what people here are like."

As if on cue, Evelyn popped her head around the corner. "Libtard is having a Penis Party, how wonderful." We began to disband as New Guy walked in, grabbing a doughnut from the box on the side. "Are these for everyone?" he asked, taking a bite. Alison answered for some reason while staring at his crotch. "Help yourself, it's Kyle's birthday. Everyone brings cakes in on their birthday, office rules." I went to slip away before Panicky Pete brushed past me and quipped, "Bishop's Avenue? Isn't that Billionaires' Row?" I never knew what to say when people questioned where I lived.

"Uh, it's a nice area. I live with a friend from uni. She's pretty successful."

Evelyn almost foamed with annoyance at learning I lived somewhere affluent. You could almost see the cogs turning in her mind, searching for something cruel to say.

"I'd love to come," New Guy started saying, but Evelyn hastily interrupted, "So would I!" He continued, looking confused by her eager interjection, "But I have to fly home for a wedding a few days before."

"So do I!" Evelyn exclaimed.

"You're flying back to the USA on Halloween for a wedding?" New Guy asked, smirking as he finished his doughnut.

"Yes. Imagine if it's the same wedding—we could travel together." She flicked her hair over her shoulders, placing her hand on her hip, while her eyes darted around, trying to work out how to save herself from her own stupidity.

"I doubt it—Ryan Masterson?" he said.

"Oh shucks, no, it's not." I immediately made a hasty exit from the cramped kitchenette before she deflect her embarrassment on to me. She continued loudly enough for me to hear, "I can't believe Liz has a rich girlfriend. Makes sense that she's a lesbian. Oh my, a Lizbian!" She cackled to herself, repeating the nickname every time she walked past me.

I can't even explain what type of gaslighting this was, or why I let it get to me. She was awful. Most people despised her, and even New Guy mocked her, but somehow she still managed to make me feel ridiculous. It was constant. I had no idea why she targeted me specifically. Perhaps because I was doing her job better than she could. Maybe she thought that by chipping away at my confidence, she'd silence me and stop me from outing her as a fraud. Bit by bit, she eroded my self-esteem until I felt invisible. When she said she was coming to the party, why couldn't I just say, "You're not invited." But I couldn't. I'd just step back and let her ruin my party as well as my work week.

Alison was excited that New Guy "would love" to come to my party, calling it an auspicious day, conveniently forgetting that I'd forwarded a phallic illustration to my boss. She was also overlooking the fact that he was just being polite. "Who gets married on Halloween—the Addams Family?" I said, and as soon as I did, I felt sad. Even after everything Gomez had said and done, a part of me still believed there was goodness in him.

Anyway, thankfully, no one from the office came to the party.

15

November 5th, 2012

New Guy had been back in the US for a few weeks, so I was genuinely surprised when I arrived at work and saw him stepping out of a town car. I smiled far more than I should have. "I've saved a few up," he said as our steps converged. The doors closed, and he began, "Alien invasion or zombie apocalypse?"

"I'd take zombies. You don't know how advanced the aliens are, and at least you know where you stand with a zombie. What's your choice?"

"I'd go with aliens. Someone I know has a friend who's an astrophysicist, and she believes there's no possibility of alien life."

"Wow, I really walked into that one!" I wanted to playfully shove his arm, but I was too awkward for anything so tactile.

It was pathetic how much his return uplifted my mood for the entire week. I spent the day sneaking glances at him across the office, grinning like a schoolgirl.

It was a good day. Evelyn was off sick, so the office was free of her pestilence. New Guy was back, and Johnson had smacked his groin on the corner of Spanish Marcus' desk. It was also Rose's birthday, so the girls and I went for a few cheeky wines at lunch, and we didn't bother going back to the office. It was actually a great day.

I walked down the lane, a little tipsy, excited to get home for more wine. Because it was winter, it was dark both when I left for work and when I got home. I wasn't paying attention, so I didn't notice Veruschka hiding in the shadows behind her fence. It was six degrees; had she been waiting in the cold just for me? She started with her usual favourites. "It's not right what goes on in that house." Then she said something so bizarre that I couldn't stop thinking about it. "You don't remember your nightmares because you're living in one." At first, I laughed; it was so melodramatic. She kept shouting as I walked away, the streetlights flickering with her torrid energy. But later, I lay awake that night. I could never remember my dreams—not everyone does, as Mad had said. I knew better than to listen to anything Veruschka said, but I was gullible.

November 7th, 2012

Mad walked into the library where I was working on a jigsaw puzzle. "That's why you're single," she sniped, before walking back out again.

November 9th, 2012

I woke up with a pounding headache. It was the quarterly meeting, and they were too important to miss for a sick day. I scrambled through every junk drawer and cabinet looking for tablets, but there wasn't a single medicine in the entire castle. I poked my head around Mad's bedroom door and quietly whispered her name. She grumbled, "What is it?" and put a pillow over her head. I looked at her dressing table, littered with expensive makeup, much of which was crumbled on the carpet and sprayed up the wall. I saw a selection of small tablet bottles, one labelled "headache tablets." I popped two in my mouth, reached for the glass of water on Mad's desk, and took a swig—which turned out to be vodka. "Vile creature," I muttered as I ran downstairs to find actual water.

A fuss over Dandy, a wave to Rory as he pootled past in his Mini (he never offered me a lift), power-walk to the tube—armpits, escalators, no coffee today. I never knew what to believe; some say coffee helps headaches, others say it makes them worse. Better to stick to water, so I picked up a cold bottle from the station shop. By the time I reached the office, the headache had migrated to a strange pressure behind my eyes. I worried it was the start of blurry vision and a monster migraine.

I slung my jacket and bag on my chair and headed straight for the meeting room. The lights seemed especially bright, and my mouth was unusually dry. The next thing I remember was a massive rush, like a power surge up the back of my neck, fuelling every nerve in my brain. My head slumped forward, hitting the table. My head felt too heavy to lift. The voices around me sounded like they were at the end of a cave, shouting down to me. Evelyn's shrill voice echoed in the distance, "Oh look, she died from her own boredom."

Someone lifted my head, and I slowly regained consciousness. It was New Guy, saying, "Elizabeth, can you hear me?" As I opened my eyes, he jolted back, going "Whoa." My pupils had dilated to double their usual size. "Have you taken anything?" he asked, holding me upright as I'd turned into a floppy rag doll. I looked into his deep brown eyes and started stroking his left arm like he was a kitten. I knew exactly what I'd taken. "Call Mad," I managed to say, still stroking his arm.

Alison returned with my phone and asked for my password. The screen was so bright the pixels looked like fireworks. Alison called Mad. "She wants to know if you've taken anything?" I replied, "Headache pills."

She went away and then came back. "How many?" I held up two fingers and watched my hand as it seemed to blow in the wind.

Alison returned to New Guy and said, "We need to get her up and downstairs." "Is she okay?" he asked, helping me stand. "She'll be fine. It was just something she ate." As she said it, she gave me a death stare, mouthing "MOLLY." I couldn't help but laugh. Of course, it was. They called for the lift, but I tapped my toe on the newly arrived floor, deeming it unsafe. The thought of getting into the elevator, which I'd ridden every day without issue, suddenly seemed too horrific.

"No death tunnel," I announced. Facing my colleagues, I whispered, "They can't be trusted."

The only other option was the stairs. New Guy offered to help me down, his arm wrapped around mine. Each step had to be felt with my foot before I trusted it to hold me. I couldn't judge the depth of the next step, and it took an excruciating amount of time to reach the bottom. In the 40 minutes it took us to descend all fifteen floors, I told New Guy he smelled like George Clooney looked, that I'd never been in love, and that I was sad I never finished Rats for Dinner. On the last flight, I started stroking his chest and waist while singing a (in my opinion) rather pitchy rendition of Kate Bush's "Wuthering Heights."

Mad was waiting at the bottom of the staircase, looking penitent, with Thomas by her side. I was guided towards Thomas while Mad stayed back to thank New Guy and apologise. I managed to hold off from being sick until we got back home. The rest of the afternoon was a rollercoaster of calamity, euphoria, angst, and vomiting. Mad, being the friend she is, decided the best way to help was to get mashed as well, so she took two "headache pills" and joined me.

Thomas stayed for an hour or two before deciding it was all too much of a mess. I remember snippets. We sat in two velour wingback chairs on opposite sides of the entrance hall, shouting questions at each other—at least, I think I was shouting; everything felt loud. I was aware I was talking unusually fast. It felt like the day was set out in movie frames. We'd move rooms, change pace, pause briefly when the wave crashed or when one of us was sick. The last thing I remember is telling Mad I didn't trust Jude, to which she replied, "I've never lived on a yacht." We eventually fell asleep fully clothed in an empty bathtub, with Bingo sprawled between us, each of us cradling a bottle of water.

The next day I woke to a mass of unread messages and emails, none of which I could face. I knew I had to read them—I wanted to know how bad it was—but my fragile state wasn't ready for the consequences. The silver lining (and I had to dig deep to find one in this mess) was that it was Friday. I didn't know if I'd still have a job on Monday. If I did, I'd probably be having several inappropriate conduct meetings with Alison, and at worst, New Guy might file a harassment complaint. It was the trifecta of screw-ups: feeling up your hot boss, turning up to work out of your mind on MDMA, and tripping balls in front of all your coworkers. All before 10 a.m.

I didn't even open the curtains. I called for Bingo to be my emotional support, but his loyalty was tested when Rory came by to walk him and check on us. He brought us sandwiches, but I couldn't face eating. “Rory, I can never go back there” I said, holding out my arm like an elderly Victorian dying of Cholera.

"Thomas handled everything. You've been signed off for the week with 'high-grade hallucinogenic fever.'"

"Does that exist?"

"Sort of."

"Would that explain me touching up my boss?"

"Nothing could explain that, except your wanton libido."

Around 3 p.m., I finally crawled into Mad's room. She was sitting up watching cartoons but kindly muted them when I entered, seeing my aversion to sound.

"Why did you label MDMA as headache tablets?!"

"Because it seemed less uncouth than having a vial labelled 'ecstasy' in my chambers. Also, I didn't expect anyone to help themselves."

"You were asleep! You said, 'eerhghhghhhhghhh.'"

"You're welcome to anything in this house, but maybe next time, check."

“There won't be a next time. I'm not going back.”

“I fully support this decision. You don't need to surround yourself with toxicity for £200 a day. You're not a prostitute. Take some time, be creative. Find yourself.” She unmuted her show and, in an attempt at comfort, awkwardly cupped the crown of my head.

I was already signed off for the week, so I figured if I was leaving, I might as well extend it to two weeks before mustering the courage to quit. It took about three days to start feeling remotely normal again, two of which I spent refreshing my emails, looking for any sign of concern or mockery—but neither came. I thought about writing to the New Guy to apologise, but I couldn't find the courage. The weather mirrored my mood: constant rain and grey skies. I spent the first week rewatching *Sex and the City*, only leaving my room to let Bingo out to chase wildlife between snack runs. In week two, I dusted off an old Mega Drive I found in the lounge and brought it upstairs. Supplies were dwindling, so I messaged Thomas to ask if he'd mind picking up some groceries on his way home. This resulted in Rory, Thomas, and Madeleine standing at the foot of my bed, staging an intervention. Even the dogs seemed against me. They took turns lecturing me. (Not the dogs).

"You can't just fester in your room forever," began Rory. Madeleine continued, "I know I said you didn't need a job, but I didn't expect the alternative to be you turning into some bedroom gremlin, sneaking downstairs for titbits like a rat in a Moroccan souk."

"I'm just taking some time. I'm figuring out other avenues."

"You have countless avenues, yet your motivation seems confined to this cesspit."

I had always thrived under structure, driven by deadlines and guidelines. I wasn't used to commanding my own day—which is why my book, my illustrations, and my compositions all remained unfinished. I was only ever good at following instructions.

Mad continued, “I'm a big advocate of owning your situation. By hiding away here, you're just letting yourself wither.” She paused, flinging open the curtains. But the weather was so dismal that the room stayed as dim as before. “You're letting people like Evelyn win. You need to go back and prove they can't hurt you. You are brilliant, Elizabeth, and it infuriates me that you crumble at the first sign of difficulty. You can't just run away because you made a mistake.”

Rory and Thomas gave a small golf clap, and Madeleine curtsied. “Honestly, some people live as if they're not the main character in their own story.”

She spun her head back towards me, like an owl. “This is your life. You don't get another one, so stop acting like this is a warm-up. Get out of bed, NOW, have a goddamn shower, and get dressed.” From across the room, Thomas, feeling redundant for not having participated in the lecture, nervously chimed in, “And would it kill you to put on some bloody makeup?”

“Fine. I didn't realise having a bit of time to myself was so upsetting for everyone.” The clapping intensified as I stood up.

16

I woke up early to go back to work, making a bit more effort to look presentable, and ensuring I didn't draw further attention to myself by being late. I was so early I didn't even see Dandy for a fuss. The office was eerily quiet. I wasn't used to being one of the first in. I wanted to hide behind my computer, catch up on work, and let things settle down. I went to get a coffee. As soon as I stepped into the kitchenette, I saw New Guy with his back to me, making a drink.

I died inside. I had hoped to delay this interaction for as long as possible. It would look even worse if I turned around and left. Just as I inhaled to speak, he cut in, not yet seeing who was behind him. Either he saw my reflection in the kettle, or he was a sexy clairvoyant.

“Johnson James isn't his real name,” he began, as he poured boiling water into his mug. “He changed it about 25 years ago.” He stirred his drink and placed the spoon calmly on the worktop. He turned slowly, checking no one else was in earshot. “His actual name is Johnson Fondler.” He smirked, raising an eyebrow. “But you didn't hear that from me,” he said as he glided out of the room.

I’d never been in love before, but that moment was how I imagined it felt.

Evelyn strode in from the lift, arm in arm with Johnson like high school besties. I kept my gaze firmly on my computer as she announced, almost shouting, “Look who's back!” She looked genuinely excited; she must have been lonely over the past fortnight without anyone to humiliate. Johnson, who must have been working two jobs in my absence, bore an expression of both relief and fury. It looked like he was making his way over to give me grief, so I stood and made my way to the morning meeting, taking the long route to avoid him.

Before everyone was seated, it was just me, Karen, Panicky Pete, and Rose in the room, before Evelyn and Johnson skidded in. Rose, sounding genuinely concerned, asked how I was feeling.

"Overtly tactile, I believe," chimed Evelyn, looking to Johnson, who joined her in mocking laughter.

"I'm much better," I replied. "Just to clear the air, I was having a dreadful day and had a high fever, but I wasn't tactile beyond boundaries. I don't want anyone to think I'm some sort of..." I paused, turning to Johnson, "Fondler." He cocked his head bemusedly, like Bingo does when he doesn't understand whether we've said "walkies" or not. I lifted my eyebrows to let him know I knew. Evelyn opened her spiteful mouth to continue, but before she could finish, Johnson Fondler said, "We're just glad to have you back, aren't we, Evelyn?" Evelyn looked just as shocked as I was. It wasn't the end of the maltreatment, but it was enough to bury the whole "coming to work melted" episode.

Tip-tap, tip-tap down the corridor—Daphne entered, followed by New Guy. "Elizabeth," she declared before taking her place at the front of the table. "You've been noticeably missed. We're pleased to have you back."

This was a good day. Or so I thought. When the meeting ended, Evelyn stood behind my chair, waiting while everyone filed out. Alison caught my eye, shaking her head. I shrugged, silently asking what she meant, but she started typing something on her phone. Not soon enough, though. As New Guy was about to pass, Evelyn audibly 'whispered' to him, "You left these at my apartment the other day."

I couldn't see what she handed him, but a message popped up from Alison: "Ignore it. Nothing happened; it's just her plan to upset you." Why anyone would go to such lengths was beyond me. I ignored it, which only seemed to enrage her further. "We should have mandatory drug tests," she muttered, but everyone had already left. I jolted my chair back, forcing her to move, and whispered, "You're unravelling," as I walked out. This was the closest I had come to a win—though it only seemed to frustrate the Demogorgon and open the gates of hell.

November 27th, 2012

I was going over an eloquent piece about the recent election scandal, written by a journalist I hadn't yet met, Sue Dinym. It turned out to be New Guy, who still liked to write the odd article incognito. When Rose pointed out it was a play on 'pseudonym', I felt a bit foolish. IT Adam called out across the office, "Who is working on electiongate?" I raised a hand. A few minutes later, an email notification popped up from 'Michael Jackson'. It really amused me. As it turns out, it wasn't the King of Pop, but the private investigator who worked for the publication. I agreed to meet him on my lunch break at The Worlds End. He certainly didn't look like Michael Jackson. He was a short, stout man in his early forties, dressed like he was stuck in the nineties—bootleg jeans, a leather jacket, and dyed, thick black hair gelled into a bouffant. He handed over an envelope of photos, and when he asked if I was staying for a drink, I took the opportunity to see if he offered his services for private matters. I wanted to see if he could abate my suspicions of Jude. When I asked what I could expect him to charge, he said, "If you rub my lamp, then out of boundless gratitude, I will grant you wishes three."

"By lamp, are you referring to your penis?"

"Yes."

"How about you grant me one wish, I pay for these drinks, and I don't report you to HR for sexual harassment."

"Deal," he said, holding out a clammy-looking hand, which I was reluctant to shake.

Michael Jackson followed Jude Peters for two weeks. He went through his bins, hacked into his emails, and went through his tax returns. He was as clean as the Queen's cutlery. There was nothing suspicious about Jude Peters. He donated to charity, authored poems for his wife, ate vegan, loved his mother, and flossed twice a day.

I still didn't trust him.

"You, however," he continued. "A twenty-four-year-old postgrad on 45k a year, living in a £100 million house."

Say what you want about Michael Jackson, but he is a meticulous private eye.

December 2nd, 2012

Evelyn took the long way around the office so that she passed by me first, casually tossing a USB stick onto my desk, which missed my coffee by centimetres. She then teetered over to New Guy's office, and I knew she was trying to cause a scene. I stood up and started walking over to the kitchenette.

"So, I'll get my driver to pick you up tomorrow at 6 pm." She bellowed it so loudly that New Guy almost fell back in his chair from surprise. I came back out with some of Rose's birthday cake, and once more, for the cheap seats at the back, she announced, "So I'll come and get you tomorrow at 6 pm," New Guy looking at her, like the madwoman she is.

I'm ashamed to say that her efforts worked. But rather than pangs of unrequited heartbreak, I felt disappointment. I thought he would be better than that. She's obviously beautiful, and I understood why men would initially find her appealing, but surely not once they got to know her? His judgement couldn't be that impaired that he didn't recognise her as repugnant. I don't know why I imagined he would be different from other men; I didn't even know him properly. It just felt like he had more substance, yet I was clearly no good judge. I didn't have a great track record.

I arrived home to find the fire roaring; M was curled up with Bingo watching *Police Academy 1-6*. I slumped on the sofa as Bingo shuffled over to clamber onto my lap. “What's the matter with you?” asked Mad in response to my massive huff.

“I think New Guy is shagging the antichrist.”

“Elizabeth, have you ever asked this man on a date?!”

“You know the answer to this. He's out of my league, and he's never asked me out either.”

“He's your boss! I don't imagine he's allowed to just walk around hitting on his underlings at whim. I'm sure even you can figure that out.”

“So what am I supposed to do, stand in his doorway during office hours and see if he wants to flirt a little?”

“You act as if you're not in control of anything that affects your life. You have a degree in philosophy, for goodness' sake. Surely you know the answers to some of these questions? Arrange drinks with some of your office friends and casually invite him along.”

“It's too late now; he's in love with Evil Lynn.”

Madeleine raised her elbow to her forehead and fell back into the sofa, pretending to faint. “It's all so dramatic! I doubt he's in love. You've convinced yourself you're the victim for so long that you're becoming one. That witch needs to be drowned. It's ruined your day, and now it's ruining our evening. I'm going to fetch us some wine, and you can watch the last three films with me. By the time I get back, you need to change that attitude.”

December 20th, 2012

It was the last day of work for the year. Everything felt more positive when it was Christmas. People were more generous and in high spirits, the streets twinkled with festive lights, shop windows covered in snow, and a scent of cinnamon filled the air. A light dusting of snow fell, and suddenly everything felt like a Dickensian scene. Except if Ebenezer Scrooge had leant out of his Cornhill townhouse, saying, “You boy, what day is this?” he'd be told to F off.

Everyone was going all out with the ugly Christmas jumpers, except for Evelyn, who dressed as Mrs Santa (if Mrs Santa was turning tricks at the North Pole). Alison asked David Wong to change after his "HO HO HO" jumper with a picture of a pole dancer offended the older crowd. Rose hung mistletoe near the lift and belly laughed every time someone walked underneath it, but no one paid any attention.

We all gathered in the meeting room to open our Secret Santa gifts with a glass of cheap Asti. The paper really splashed out this year! They blamed the lack of an official work party on the financial collapse, offering a few office drinks instead—namely, some £3-a-bottle Asti. There was a big pile of gifts on the table, and everyone crammed themselves in while Alison divvied out the presents. It was obvious whether the purchaser was male or female, old or young—lots of soaps and candle sets, as well as some 'quirky' edible underwear and body chocolate.

I opened mine. No one was looking at me, as Ed held up a chocolate penis, and so all eyes were on him. I had a box of weight loss pills. I pushed them back into the wrapper and tossed them in the bin. "What did you get?" bellowed Evelyn from across the room. I just walked out and went to the bathroom so that my tears weren't seen. I'd been looking forward to the work drinks, and now I just wanted to go home. I listened to the raucous crowd gathering in the corridor, waiting to descend to The World's End. Alison tried to call twice, but I let it ring out and waited until I couldn't hear any more noise from outside. I just wanted to go home.

I knew I was letting her win. I was angry at myself for allowing her to have an effect and ruin the one night out when everyone goes for a drink. When I got to the tube station, I looked over at the pub, and for a second, I was tempted to just go. The thought of spending any more time in the same room as her made me recoil. A text message from Spanish Marcus arrived. It was a Photoshop of Evelyn being in hell, receiving a piece of coal. I sent back a '□'. It made me sad. There were so many good eggs; I would have spent more time with everyone if it weren't for her. She insisted on going to these things just to make it unbearable for me so that I wouldn't go. I wondered her reasons and remembered Alison's words—she needed to keep me constrained and afraid, so that I would never let her secret slip that she had no talent. It felt good to have these thoughts; anger was a prouder state than shame. A second twinge to just go in there, but I couldn't muster the courage. I sat on the tube, watching various office parties giggling and laughing, and felt so disappointed.

17

I arrived home and could hear swing music from the end of the driveway. The house came alive at Christmas. Every single tree shone with twinkling lights, and all the chimneys were puffing out smoke. I opened the door and heard murmurings from the library. Most of the people from our road were there, together with Madeleine's science crew, (not Jude), some of the band, and, of course, Rory and Thomas. Mad was beaming! She was walking around pouring champagne, and when she saw me, she galloped towards me at the same pace as Bingo, and they both wriggled with glee. “I've received the funding and approval to start human stage testing of my microchip!”

“Madeleine, this is huge.”

“You bet it's huge! It's Nobel Prize huge. There's good news and bad news. Bad news is I will be in the USA for quite some time at the beginning, but good news, I've got us a plane to Los Angeles, and we can go to VEGAS for New Year's.” It was so much to process, but this wasn't about me. I was so pleased for her; I wasn't going to be a fun sponge and ruin her insane happiness! So, I agreed to go, taking the flute of champagne, drinking it in one, and then extending it for an immediate refill. “Let's celebrate!”

I flew back from LAX with a stopover at JFK. As I flew in, I saw all the famous landmarks from the first-class seat that Mad swore were from her air miles, I was tempted to head straight out and spend a few days in New York. Instead, I had to go back to work in two days, back to reality. I had three weeks away to regroup, sightsee, eat, drink, gamble, shop, and swim. I wish I felt rejuvenated, but I felt like I could use another holiday to get over this one.

I wandered around the airport, peering out of every window trying to catch a glimpse of places I recognised. I bought an overpriced I HEART NY T-shirt, an Empire State keyring, and a deli bagel with an apple pie milkshake, which didn't give me change from $100. The gate to my flight was announced, and I checked for the time on the Cartier watch that Mad got me for Christmas. We promised that we weren't doing gifts this year. Our gift to each other was going halves on a helicopter ride to the Grand Canyon, but the little swine didn't follow the rules.

I heard her piercing voice before I saw her, which made me hang back and shudder in horror. There were four flights a day going to the UK and so many days that they could have been flying back. I played enough poker to understand odds, and the probability that they would be on THE SAME FLIGHT as me was ridiculous. I could avoid seeing them, it would be fine. I hovered back and did some shopping, waiting for the call to board. I looked around and couldn't see them anymore. When first class was called to board, I walked down to the plane without seeing anyone. They weren't in first class, which had all boarded, so that was one relief. If they were sat next to me, I think I would have just walked off. Having to kill thirty-five minutes and buying a Valentino handbag was probably not the most mature way to deal with my nerves. I pulled my hood up and put in my headphones, before covering my face with a book. Passengers started shuffling past to get to their seats and started stopping by me as they waited for people to faff around, stowing their overhead luggage further down. I felt someone glaring down at me, and I told myself not to look, but I just couldn't help myself. It was New Guy. Evelyn was standing in front of him. I shook my head and put my finger to my lips, gesturing a thumb at Evil and shaking my head again. He understood, but mouthed, 'Nice to see you,' and smiled, before Evil started shouting at the elderly, disabled lady in front of her to 'get a move on.' I didn't smile back. I went back to looking out of the window. I felt angry with him.

It's strange how perception plays such a large part in lusting over someone. I'd lost all respect for New Guy, based on his choice of companionship. Even those brief few seconds of her shouting at someone on a plane should have been enough to make him recoil at her character. Why would you choose to affiliate with someone that loathsome? And if that was the type of person whose company he entertained, then he certainly wasn't the person I thought he was. His network was not one I'd ever want to associate with. I took a deep breath as well as a free glass of champagne from the kind flight attendant. The plane took off over the north of the city, and just as the sun disappeared behind the skyscrapers, so too did my New Guy crush. It felt liberating. I knew what I had to do. I would start this New Year with a new outlook. I couldn't let these parasites ruin me.

June 2013

It was the first time Mad had been home since she left. I was so bored that I even went back to see my family. Predictably, my dad's cheap office romance lasted less than six months, and within a year, my mum took him back. It was the most desperate display of weakness I'd ever seen. No wonder I couldn't tackle my own demons if this was my heritage. They bickered over the smallest things, and when I asked why they were so horrible to each other, they just laughed it off. "We're just playing," they chuckled, one fake laugh following another. I knew I'd made a huge mistake coming back. They'd both given up trying to improve their lives; it was easier to fall back into old habits. My father probably thought it was financially sensible to cohabit and split the bills, while my mother tried to sell me the nonsense that "true love always finds its way home." Neither of them seemed happy or had anything in common. If this was true love, maybe I was better off alone.

I tried dating a few times. People would suggest, "You should meet my friend (insert lonely pervert here), he's so nice." "Nice" was usually dull, or ugly. Once it was both. I had to set some guidelines for myself, and not settling had to be one of them. I couldn't become my parents. I was earning more money but had no Mad to spend it with, so I started going to all the restaurants Evelyn was being paid to review and added a few more to my own blog. I watched all the new shows, either alone or with anyone I could persuade from work. If they were camp or fabulous, I'd invite Rory and Thomas.

Every now and then, I offered myself as a session pianist in exchange for tickets. The best part was they always agreed, but rarely called in the favour. Sometimes, I'd just correct the grammar and spelling in Evelyn's articles, yet when they reached print, they were always reworked by The Fondler. Say what you like about that malevolent little bottom feeder, but the man could write. Why he kept Evelyn on all this time was beyond me. He was like her pet, riding on her coattails like a desperate puppy. Another victim of an unfulfilling marriage—perhaps she was sleeping with him.

Her attempts to make me miserable continued, but I was becoming immune to her awfulness. She had no interest in doing her job properly, and it baffled me how someone could have so little pride. She set low personal standards, then constantly failed to meet them. The more I ignored her, the more she tried to provoke me—ordering coffee for everyone in the office except me, bringing everyone a slice of birthday cake and saying, "Best you don't have any," when she reached my desk. Rose and Spanish Marcus would mime stabbing her with a biro. He photoshopped her holding a three-tiered cake with a speech bubble saying, "No joy for you, peasant." He was a rose amongst the thorns. Despite her, I still enjoyed my job, even if I got no credit for the content I wrote, which Evelyn continually leeched off.

The longer Mad was away, the more I realised I couldn't rely on her forever. We spoke via emails and messages every day, but it wasn't the same. Our friendship was so special, but I found myself depending on her for my happiness. That was proved true when I went home on the evening of September 6th and found her there. We both screamed with excitement! I was startled when she ran towards me; I thought she was going to hug me, but instead she handed me a Long Island Iced Tea like a relay baton.

"Why didn't you tell me you were coming home?"

"I wanted it to be a surprise! We've had such an overwhelming number of volunteers for the programme, we're just waiting for the official go-ahead for the next phase of human trials before we explore commercial applications."

"What? I thought clinical trials took years?"

"They do, but this isn't a drug. It's a removable chip, so there are no permanent chemical changes. It's like putting on a pair of headphones, but medically implanted in your brain, like a pacemaker."

She was so animated and enthusiastic; I'd never seen her this positive.

"And also, there's this." She extended her ring finger, and I got a little overexcited. It wasn't an engagement ring, but a promise ring. Apparently, it meant Lucas was promising she was "the one he would marry one day." She seemed so content. I really liked Lucas; he was one of the good ones. Anyone who could turn the stone-cold Madeleine Magdalene into a believer in true love had my approval. She told me how he'd flown out to meet her, how they'd gone to Disneyland, and how it was now her favourite place in the world. They'd walked along Venice Beach promenade, where Lucas encouraged her to use the Zoltar machine from *Big*. When the card fell, it read, "Madeleine, there isn't anyone I could love as much as I love you." As she told me this, tears welled up in both our eyes.

When she asked what I'd been up to, I had nothing to say. I'd done nothing. Mad had been living an incredible adventure, while I was stuck here, living the same fresh hell, day after day. Veruschka was right. I *was* living in a nightmare. I didn't want to ruin Mad's buzz, so I didn't tell her I was miserable. She'd only tell me that I was the only one who could control my happiness, and she'd be right. I was so far down the rabbit hole, feeling completely helpless.

"Have you seen anything of Jude? He promised to check on you."

"Mad, he hates me, and he hates this house. He acts like it's a portal to the underworld and I am the damned."

"You're so dramatic! He's been instrumental in helping me with my research. He's a genius. Geniuses aren't famous for their congeniality. We need to catch up, Bethy; there are two loungers on that balcony and two bottles of fizz with our names on them. Okay, maybe three. Maybe four."

By 10 pm, we were singing *Bohemian Rhapsody* at full volume, so loudly that Thomas messaged to say he could hear us from his house. By midnight, we were dancing to Blondie in the ballroom. At 1 am, we were back on the balcony, tears flowing—happy tears. The sky was full of shooting stars, a rare meteor shower that seemed to appear just for us. It was a good night.

I went back to work on Monday with a spring in my step. I left the house, walked up the lane, and waved at Rory as he drove past. Why does he never offer me a lift? I saw Petra, but no Dandy. I looked at her, and tears welled up in her eyes. I didn't ask what had happened; I could already tell. I gave her a big hug, the type I'd give Dandy, and we stood in the street sobbing. "Seeing you was his favourite time of day," she said, making me feel even more grief-stricken. "He was a good boy." We nodded in agreement. Tube station, tube tears, coffee, too sad for pastries.

When I got to work, everyone around my desk looked at me sheepishly. Spanish Marcus left his desk as soon as I arrived. I looked up at Rose to say good morning, and she looked terrified. She looked down at her computer and said nothing. Very confusing. I checked my reflection in the computer monitor, worried I had some horrifying face from all the crying. Pete caught my eye as he walked past, put his hand on my shoulder, and whispered, "I'm so sorry." I was utterly baffled. It all began to make sense when my computer loaded up and I checked my emails.

TO: ALL

Our very own Evelyn Porter has received not only a nomination at the prestigious British Journalism Awards but also a nomination in the Criticism category for the highly esteemed Pulitzer Prize for her article submissions in our sister New York publication. Management will be joining her next Friday night at the awards ceremony, but everyone is cordially invited to a champagne toast beforehand to celebrate this remarkable achievement and wish her luck.

Johnson

I stared at the email for a good few minutes before Alison walked over. "Are you okay?" I didn't mean to snap at her, but she was the first on the scene. "Of course I'm not okay! I need to get out of here before she arrives because I'm worried I'm going to beat her to death with my laptop. You saw me; you didn't see me. I went home sick. I just don't care anymore." I saw her sad face and said sorry. But even that didn't come out as intended. I was so angry.

The lift was on its way up, and I just knew it would be her and her pathetic followers when the doors opened. I took the stairs. I'd never felt this angry before. Compounded by my already awful morning, I couldn't believe this was happening. In a trance-like state, I began an autopilot walk home. I squeezed my eyes shut every now and then to refocus, trying to see where I was, not remembering the steps I'd taken before. My phone began to ping with messages. I now understood why people just lobbed their phones in the river in moments like this, but I couldn't handle the hassle of buying a new one. So, I just switched it off. I didn't need to explain myself to anyone. If they had to ask, they weren't close enough to understand.

It felt like I blinked, and I was home, feeling weary and defeated. Madeleine was already at the door with Bingo. Alison must have given her the heads-up. "I'm fine," I said, squeezing past her. "No, you're not." She did something completely out of character and pulled me in for a hug. That alone sent me into a spiral of emotion. Once I started crying, I just couldn't stop. Everything poured out, like a dam bursting—the bullying, the loneliness, the feeling of failure, the lack of control. Mad led me into the kitchen, where she pointed out that she'd made us "lunch." She'd opened whatever jars we had in the fridge and decanted them into ramekins—pickles, mustard, jam, capers, and mayo. She'd opened a tin of tuna and tipped it into a bowl. Some old pepperoni was dotted around the plate, along with some dubious cheese neither of us remembered buying, cut into cubes. Served with a stale roll and Jammie Dodgers. It was as if a seven-year-old had attempted a charcuterie.

We transferred the "banquet" to the balcony, where I discreetly fed titbits to Bingo when Mad wasn't looking. We drank beer, which was unusual. Presumably, Mad didn't want me getting too drunk too fast. She always said, "Drink when you're happy, never when you're sad." Apparently, beer was too weak to count as alcohol. She must have seen people having nuts with their beer and tried to replicate it by bringing up two egg cups, one with sultanas and another with walnuts. She acted like it was her first time on Earth and she was trying desperately to pass as human. She was clearly worried; she'd rarely made this much effort. I managed to calm down, but I was still so angry I didn't know what to do with myself.

"How did I let it get this far?"

"Which part?"

"All of it! Do you know how much I dreamed of one day having my work recognised by the BJA? And the Pulitzers!"

"You couldn't win the Pulitzer, though; you're not an American citizen."

"But still, the recognition! This repulsive person has stolen my life! She takes credit for my work, she took the guy I liked, she stops me from socialising with anyone from work, and she torments me whenever she can. I don't even know if it's all her doing anymore. I've just given up. I can't even be bothered to try." And there it was—the admission I hadn't been able to make before.

"How could I let one person oppress me to the point of giving up hope?"

"You could resolve all of this in one swoop. Tell your actual boss everything. Show her all your articles, all the originals. Tell her about the Dick Fondler. Stand up for yourself and expose her!"

"I don't have your confidence! I guarantee that as soon as I go in to work, I'll chicken out, or she'll call Johnson in, he'll deny everything, and remind her that she's the boss's daughter."

"Elizabeth, you talk about this like it's the only conflict you'll ever face. There are hundreds of Evelyns and Johnsons out there, all waiting to be complete arseholes for no reason. You let Gomez walk all over you, and now you're letting them do the same. This isn't about the person or the situation—you need to start driving your own train before it derails and explodes."

"I know what you're saying, and I agree with you. But I get anxious. I hate conflict and confrontation. I grew up watching my parents argue all the time, so I avoid any form of disagreement."

"I don't want to bully you. I wish you'd let me unleash on them for you. Part of me wants to pop the neuro chip in you for a day so you can see what it could be like if you stood up for yourself."

She downed the rest of her beer and reached into the cooler for two fresh bottles.

"Let's do it."

"Do what?"

"Let me have a go. At this point, I don't have much to lose."

"I wouldn't let you do it until we've completed every person on the trial."

"But you've done it? You and your team?"

"Yes, but we're not as important as you."

"Mad, I considered throwing myself and my phone off a bridge earlier. I don't think it gets much worse than this. If you invented it, then I trust you'd make sure nothing bad happened to me. I haven't slept properly in ages. I feel so bored, but I don't have the energy to do anything. I don't even remember the last time I felt genuinely happy before last night. In fact, when I don't have to work, I don't even bother getting dressed anymore. I feel like I just want to fall asleep and never wake up."

Mad looked at me, then at Bingo. "Give me a couple of days. I need to think about this."

Madeleine went to her lab the next morning and didn't come out again until Thursday. She came into the lounge and curled up on the sofa, looking exhausted.

"You've had time to think about this now you're sober. Are you sure you want to go through with it?"

"I haven't even had the courage to switch my phone back on. I've spent the last two days eating toasted sandwiches and watching *Judge Judy*. I think it's time I took some positive action."

"Okay. We've set everything up to start on Saturday. You can eat anything you like up to midnight the night before, but don't drink any liquids past 6:30 am. Have you had general anaesthetic before?"

"Once, when I was fifteen, to have my tonsils out. I woke up and it was like it hadn't happened."

"This time, you'll wake up and everything will look and feel the same, but there'll be subtle differences. You'll embellish and omit certain details, but it'll be just as you imagine it. You'll get up, have a shower, get dressed. Everything will smell and look the same. It'll even feel the same when you need the loo. But you'll be in control. It's your imagination driving this ship."

"Can I imagine Evelyn getting hit by a bus?"

"I don't think that'll help your spiritual awakening. This isn't about her; it's about you. You'll do the things you wish you could do if you weren't, well, you. Everyone who used the experience negatively came out feeling unfulfilled. It's not something you get to experience more than once—for now, anyway. So use it wisely."

"And what happens when I want to come out?"

"The chip will be removed exactly six hours after it's implanted. A day in real life is about a month in the simulation. So far, the shortest test subject lasted two days. Six hours is ridiculously safe. As a marker, we'll play a song every 45 minutes to mark the start of a new day. I'll play my alarm song—I know you love it."

"Okay. And you're sure there aren't any complications?"

"The only person with any complication so far was me. On the first go, it took me a few minutes to come around, but that's only because I have a busy mind and a vivid imagination. I wasn't sure what was real and what wasn't until the anaesthetic wore off, but within an hour, I was fine."

"On the first go?"

"I've been in five more times, and there were no further problems. And let's face it, your creativity isn't great. You can't even finish that cartoon about rats. No offence."

"You can't just say 'no offence' after you've said something offensive!"

"Eliza, I adore you, but ingenuity isn't one of your strongest attributes. I would never lie to you."

I turned away to sulk. "I'll finish it eventually," I muttered under my breath.

September 12th, 2013-The day of the experiment

Suddenly, as if no time had passed, I was awake again. It felt like I was floating on a cloud, surrounded by bright lights. I thought I was in heaven. I could hear voices calling my name, asking if I was okay. I wasn't sure where I was, but I knew I wasn't in Madeleine's lab anymore. I turned my head from side to side, and the lights followed. Delilah was standing over me, though she looked different. Her hair wasn't in its usual scraped-back ponytail, and she wore soft makeup. Madeleine sat beside me, gently stroking my hand. As I turned towards her, she whispered, "Welcome to Elizabeth's world!"

Once my eyes adjusted, I studied the rest of the room. "Where are we?"

"I don't know. This is your experience. Whoever is here or wherever you are is entirely your choice, remember?"

"If that's true, then why isn't Johnny Depp here?"

"Because you don't really want him here, I suppose. How are you feeling?"

"Tired, fuzzy. Dehydrated."

"May I suggest you take a drink, then close your eyes again? Make sure you truly take everything in—the smells, the sounds, the beauty of it all. Really absorb all the information your mind has stored over the years. Explore this world as though it's your first day on earth. Take the time to observe and appreciate your surroundings. It's an incredible thing to behold."

I closed my eyes.

19

I'm not even sure how long I slept, but when I awoke, everyone was gone. I checked my phone to see what day it was: 4:05 p.m., Sunday, 13th September. I tried to sit up too quickly, making myself dizzy, but it soon passed. I swung my legs around to stand and instinctively messaged Madeleine, "She rises." She replied within seconds, "I wish her a safe voyage."

I wasn't in my bedroom. In fact, I wasn't even in Madeleine's house. The room was luxurious, with plush bedding and expensive-looking furniture. Floor-to-ceiling windows ran along the entire wall, overlooking the city. Was I in a hotel?

I noticed a black and gold silk robe hanging on the wardrobe door, which I decided to put on. Only then did I realise I was wearing expensive-feeling nightwear—silk and lace shorts with a matching vest. A significant upgrade from my usual ragged Philharmonic Breasts T-shirt. I opened the wardrobe door, expecting shelves, but instead found a walk-in closet. Clearly, I made more money in this life. And I was much tidier. Neatly hung outfits, skirts, and trousers on the lower rail, tops and blazers above. On the opposite side were dresses and shirts. The rest of the space was filled with shoes and bags—an abundance of glorious shoes. I got sidetracked for quite a while before realising I still didn't know where I was.

I walked over to the window. I could see Marble Arch a few streets away. The view was astonishing. An expensive handbag was draped over the chair by the vanity table. Inside, I found my driving licence: Portman Square Penthouse. I never thought my preferred reality would involve having a place of my own, but here I was. I felt a bit sad.

After everything Madeleine and I had been through together, I messaged her saying, “I’m in Portman Square.” I knew I was essentially messaging myself, but it still felt comforting. I didn’t want to feel alone.

I made my way out of the bedroom into the main open-plan living area. I was dumbfounded by how spectacular it was. A stark contrast to Madeleine’s mansion—everything here was sleek and modern, no antiques in sight. The only thing that looked like my choice was the piano—a beautiful Bösendorfer grand, understandably taking centre stage. The floor-to-ceiling windows continued into this room, framing a sunken living space, a cinema-sized television, and, on the other side, a mini library with an egg chair and a remote-control fireplace. I moved to examine the cast-iron staircase, but the books on the glass coffee table caught my eye. “The Sound of the Soul: The Philosophy and Psychology of Music by Elizabeth Angelo.”

No. F’ing. Way.

I flicked through it, and there it was—my book, completed and bound. As I went to put it down, I noticed another Elizabeth Angelo book. An animated novella: *Rats for Dinner—The Underground Society*. I skimmed through it, and it was fantastic! Had I just finished it as I read it? A little self-indulgent of me to place my own work centre stage on the coffee table. I took them back to the bedroom—I’d have a proper read later. I climbed the stairs, hoping to find a rooftop garden, which was exactly what awaited me. A 360-degree panoramic cityscape, the kind Madeleine and I would sit and gaze at together. It was breathtaking. An outdoor sofa and fire pit, white Italian ceramic tiles, and large planters filled with an abundance of greenery—all framed by outdoor lights and a glass fence. It was incredibly cool. I walked to the corner of the terrace, overlooking Regent Street, and shouted down, “HELLO LONDON!” Someone shouted back, “FUCK OFF!”

I considered what Madeleine had told me before I was sedated. I started to notice the things I usually ignored: the city's landmarks, the lush green trees, the architecture, the tones of the setting sun, the aromas wafting up from nearby restaurants, making me peckish. I wondered if there was any wine in the fridge (there was). Then I reminded myself I should probably wait. Tomorrow would be my first day back at work. I wanted to be fresh and composed. I spent some time exploring the rest of my space, occasionally glancing back at the manuscripts in the bedroom, curious to see what a finished book of mine looked like.

I picked out my outfit for the morning, which took me over an hour. Once I started trying things on, it became addictive. There were so many beautiful clothes—things I'd never have bought for myself, things I never thought would suit me. Finally, I made my way to the study and noticed a black leather Prada work bag on the Herman Miller chair. Inside was a bound folder with articles I'd written for *The Inquirer* and the original, unedited drafts by Evelyn, all dated and filed in order, side by side. There were also printed copies of reviews I'd written for my blog that had been plagiarised by both Evelyn and Johnson Fondler over the years. I ran myself a bath and started reading my book. I never realised how important it was to me until it was physically in my hands. I knew I needed to finish it, if only to say that I had. I felt so accomplished and fulfilled. I didn't even care if anyone else had read it.

Rats for Dinner was inevitably entertaining—after all, Madeleine had written it. Random, outrageous, and unbelievable, yet beyond the hilarity, she managed to capture the underlying plight of marginalised groups in society. The rats were superior throughout; it was people who were the problem. In the end, it was clear that civilisation couldn't compare to the rats. I giggled my way to sleep, messaging Madeleine goodnight and receiving a reply. It already felt slightly less strange that the person on the other end of the phone was my imagination.

I woke up feeling fresh and full of vigour. I was excited to finally free myself from the frustrations and challenges of the past few years. I felt confident. I was showered, dressed, hair and makeup done, and all necessary evidence gathered. What I hadn't considered was how long it would take me to get to work or how I would even get there. I went downstairs, already regretting the killer stilettos. It was 7:45 a.m.—I usually wouldn't even be awake by now. As I left the lift, a smartly dressed doorman opened the entrance door, greeting me by name. "Your driver is waiting for you, Ms Angelo." Driver! How wonderful! I slid into the back of the blacked-out BMW, and the driver asked, "Straight to the office, or to Le Pâtisserie Jardin on the corner?"

"Le Jardin would be fantastic, thank you."

I arrived at the little café around the corner from work, forty-five minutes early. I had never been this early for anything in my life. The sun was shining like an August morning in Spain. The birds were in full chorus, and everyone seemed to be smiling. The air felt light, and everything was relaxing. I ordered a coffee and a croque madame. I hadn't eaten for two days, and I was ravenous. I sat back and absorbed my surroundings. Madeleine was right—the world really was beautiful if you slowed down for a moment. The toasted sandwich was the best thing I'd ever eaten. Even the coffee smelled and tasted superior. Everything felt infinitely better. I was about to face the confrontation I'd been too terrified to even consider, and I couldn't wait. I was excited, even. I left a £10 note as a tip and headed off. I was generous with my tips in this reality.

The lift doors opened, and I strode in—straight back, head held high. Hardly anyone had arrived yet. I'd hoped Daphne would be in before the morning meeting, but it was probably better to wait until afterwards anyway. I switched on my computer and saw my inbox, full of emails. Rose came over to welcome me back, commenting on how well I looked. I highlighted all the unread emails and pressed delete. She looked shocked.

"If it's important, they'll call," I said. Classic Madeleine move.

"What have I missed?" I asked, as Rose still stood in disbelief.

"There were some important deadlines in those emails," she said hesitantly.

"I couldn't care less. What have I missed?" Rose, a little confused and perhaps slightly scared, eventually said, "Johnson is annoyed that you went home. He expected you to stay and face the hypocrisy, I guess. Evelyn has convinced herself that the accolades are her own."

"Not for long," I smirked.

By saying her name, she summoned the antichrist.

I walked over to see Alison, who was on the phone, so I waved. She pointed to my outfit, nodding approvingly, mouthing, "Very nice." I continued to the meeting room, receiving compliments as people joined. When Evelyn walked in, she announced in her overly loud, patronising voice, "Someone has made an effort."

I sat upright, looked her dead in the eyes, and said, "Go fuck yourself." She looked stunned. I had always wanted to do that. She began to pretend laugh, turning to Johnson, who fake-laughed on cue. In strode the new guy, taking his place at the head of the table. He caught my eye, and I could see he was pleased to see me. He confirmed it, saying, "I'm pleased to see you." Clippety-clop. The meeting went as normal, until Daphne shuffled her papers and asked if anyone had anything to add. I piped up.

"Actually, Daphne"—I started meekly but remembered this was the new me, and I needed to speak with confidence. "Could I have a few moments of your time in private?"

Daphne nodded, and everyone began to file out. "Should I stay?" asked the new guy.

"Actually, yes, that would be great."

Johnson then said, "I should probably stay too."

"No, thank you," I replied.

I stood up, walked to their end of the table, and waited to close the door behind Johnson as he left. New Guy looked especially handsome today. I still struggled to maintain eye contact. I had rehearsed this a hundred times, but when it came to them sitting in front of me, I decided to drop the convoluted backstory and be precise and succinct. I summoned my inner Madeleine.

"I apologise for leaving so abruptly last week, but I had good reason." I handed over two folders. "For the past two years, Evelyn has been producing substandard, borderline illiterate articles, and instead of proofing them, I've been rewriting them entirely. You'll see each original draft by her on the left and the version I produced that went to print on the right. When I've been absent, Johnson has been taking reviews from my personal website and submitting them under Evelyn's name."

I paused. I could have gone on for hours about my grievances, but I needed to allow for a reaction. I didn't even mention the daily abuse I endured from her. They both skimmed the content of a few articles. New Guy raised his eyebrows—clearly, this was the first time he'd realised Evelyn's childlike intellect.

"Is Johnson aware of this?" he asked.

"He orchestrated it. When I first raised my concerns, he told me, in no uncertain terms, that if I didn't like it, I could leave. When I initially refused, he rewrote the articles himself."

Daphne hadn't said a word yet, and New Guy didn't ask anything further. After a few seconds of silence, I continued.

"Johnson implied she was the boss's daughter and that it was our job to ensure she faced no challenges in her position. But obviously, things became untenable when she was about to receive awards that rightly belong to me."

More silence.

Daphne removed her glasses and placed them on the table. "I wish you'd come to us sooner."

"I'm sorry. I wanted to. When I approached Johnson, I was silenced. Then, when you and Evelyn," I looked at the new guy, "started dating, I didn't feel I could say anything. I didn't have the courage to approach you directly. I didn't expect it to go this far. I thought either she'd leave, or Johnson would realise this couldn't continue." I began to ramble, so I stopped. I'd never seen Daphne this angry, and I started to worry it was directed at me. She turned to New Guy. He looked at her bemusedly, then back at me.

"Just for clarity, Evelyn and I have never dated." I fought back a smile because it was an obvious lie. Daphne waved dismissively as though the information was irrelevant.

"How do we handle this? Should we bring them both in here?" Daphne asked.

At this point, I interjected, "I'd rather not be here when that happens. Is that possible?"

New Guy looked up from the sheet he was reading, looking dumbfounded. "No, we wouldn't expect you to be here for that."

"What will happen?" I asked.

Daphne went to remove her glasses again before realising she wasn't wearing them. The look in her eyes was pure rage.

"At this stage, Elizabeth, all I can do is apologise. If everything you're saying is correct, this is gross misconduct in its purest form. Would you mind giving us some time to decide how to proceed? In the meantime, stay close, and if it's not already clear, we're incredibly grateful for everything you do here."

I smiled, and Daphne opened the door to let me out, calling across the room for Evelyn and Johnson. Evelyn gave me one of her self-satisfied smirks as she sauntered past. I was tempted to whisper, "Good luck," but even in a scenario of my own making, I didn't need to lower myself to her level.

I immediately emailed Alison: "Watch the meeting room. I've given Daphne all of Evil Lynn's articles."

She replied with a shocked-face emoji. I went to respond, but Daphne opened the door again to call Alison in. I pretended to work, checking emails, but I was transfixed by what was happening. Johnson looked worried, Evelyn was pointing at him and then at me, and we could hear her shouting, though nothing was audible. At one point, Daphne stood with her arms outstretched on the table, clearly at her wit's end. Alison sent me a text simply saying, "OMG." I was impatient; I wanted to know what was happening, but given the chance, I still wouldn't have stayed in the room.

I'm not sure how much time had passed—it wasn't long, maybe fifteen minutes—before the doors opened. Evelyn stormed across the office and stood so close she was practically touching my knees. She started shouting, and for a moment, I sat there and took it, until I remembered this experience was under my control. I stood up, and with my heels on, I was a good three inches taller than her. She jumped back as though she thought I'd hit her.

"You can threaten me all you like, Evelyn, but this is all your own doing. Did you really think you could silence me forever?" From her expression, it seemed she did. "Just wait until my father hears about this! You'll all be out of a job!"

I sat back down, and she continued to stand over me, issuing empty threats. It was quite amusing watching her unravel. Panicky Pete—as we called him—came over to try and intervene, standing at the far end of my desk. He wasn't near her, but she shouted, "Take your hands off me!" We held our laughter for as long as we could, and by this point, Johnson had come over to try and retrieve the fallen angel of nepotism.

Within ten minutes, she'd left the building, and I was called back into the meeting room. Daphne thanked me for coming forward, applauding my courage. Evelyn's father was mortified by the potential embarrassment to the paper if it became public. He said Evelyn had made a 'mockery' of her opportunity. They'd withdraw their Pulitzer nominations, and there was now a question mark over the UK-based award this week. Daphne said, "The BJ award that we all know you deserve." I looked at New Guy, who seemed to realise the unfortunate abbreviation at the same time. This was definitely not the time to laugh. I managed to keep a straight face and told Daphne I understood how complicated it was and didn't need the accolade. The acknowledgment alone was a huge compliment. I didn't want to drag the paper through an unnecessary retraction. I just wanted any future work to be in my name.

"We can do better than that."

Daphne stood and gestured for me to follow. She clapped her hands to get the office's attention. "Everybody, I'd like to introduce the new Editor of Entertainment, Elizabeth Angelo." My mouth dropped so wide the room could see every filling. Johnson Fondler sheepishly joined in with the applause, having just kept his job by a thread. He had no choice but to be supportive after everything he'd done. I couldn't believe it was over. All I wanted was for Evelyn to be held accountable. I could never have imagined it would lead to her being entirely removed from my life. There was whistling and cheering from my side of the room. I was so content I could burst. Would it really be this simple, I wondered?

While all this was unfolding, I felt my phone constantly vibrating in my pocket. I had eight missed calls from Mad. I stepped into the corridor to phone her back.

Screeching down the phone, her excitement garbled her words. "Slow down, Madeleine, take a breath, start again."

"The London Symphony Orchestra has norovirus."

"Oh, that's awful. All of them?" I joked.

"Yes!" she squealed, with inappropriate merriment. "They came back from a tour of Europe, and they all fell sick. That's not the best part."

"Well, it doesn't sound like there's a 'best' part."

"There's a VIP gig tonight, undisclosed guests and location. You know what that means!"

"Someone important."

"Yes!! Robert called; the band is getting back together! Valery Gergiev requested us personally."

"Shut up."

"I will not."

"I haven't performed in years! What does he want us to play?"

"Chopin – Piano Concerto No. 1 in E minor."

"MADELEINE! That's me, centre stage! Have you lost your mind? When do we have to let him know?"

"I've already let him know…." She paused. I mirrored her hesitation.

"What time does it start?" I checked my watch; it wasn't even midday. So much had happened in such a short space of time.

"They want us in South London by 4 p.m., the performance starts at 7."

"So, they're giving us two hours to rehearse?"

"Rehearse a piece we've played together a dozen times."

"I need to get back to my new apartment to see if I even have something to wear."

"No need for that, look out the window."

Mad was downstairs with the car. All I had to do now was ask for the rest of the day off after just being given a promotion. Thankfully, it was met without resistance. I think, given the circumstances, they were relieved I didn't want to pursue anything further.

The afternoon of the performance arrived, and I was the most nervous I had ever been. I hadn't played in front of an audience for years, let alone in front of unknown VIPs in an undisclosed venue. At 4 p.m., cars arrived for us. By 5 p.m., we pulled up outside St Paul's Cathedral. I gulped. It was my favourite building in London. The car door opened, and I had to swing both legs out together like a mermaid to exit, as the dress Mad had convinced me to wear was so tight I had to waddle like a penguin. Secret Service agents were searching under the car with mirrors, and a lady with a metal detector wand gave me a thorough sweep. I started choking up; this wasn't just some oligarch throwing an extravagant birthday party.

As we took to the stage for the soundcheck, Mad pulled me aside and handed me a large red velvet box. "You should wear this tonight. It was my mother's. This building deserves beauty." I opened the clasp to reveal a priceless emerald and diamond necklace. It was worth more than my family home. I considered going through the 'I can't possibly wear this, it's too valuable' spiel, but there wasn't any point. I turned around so she could fasten the vintage clasps, catching my reflection in the immaculately glossy Steinway. "It's the most beautiful piece of jewellery I've ever seen."

"Well, if you're playing Chopin in front of Barack Obama and the Royal Family, you need to look impressive." I froze. How I wished she hadn't told me that.

The ground felt unstable as I walked out on stage to the piano. I worried I wouldn't be able to play at all, given the way my hands were shaking. The orchestra followed, sitting all around me. I wasn't used to being centre stage, literally or figuratively, yet here I was, surrounded by the leader of the free world and our sovereign rulers. I turned to take in the Cathedral's magnificence, trying to absorb its beauty instead of panicking about the people staring at me. I turned back towards Mad, who was holding up her violin and bow. As soon as they began playing, I felt at ease. My surroundings blurred, and all I could hear was the music. As the strings finished their introduction, at 4 minutes 25 seconds, I began to play. For the next 40 minutes, I drifted into a world of perfect resonance. I felt calm and free of thought. It wasn't until my final note, followed by the last three strokes of the violin bow, that I realised the enormity of what had just happened.

The audience rose to their feet, applauding, whistling, and calling out 'Bravo.' I turned to embrace Valery, who whispered, "Phenomenal" in my ear. I applauded the rest of the orchestra, who tapped their sheet music with their bows before joining me at the front. I couldn't see much of the crowd as the lights were so overbearing, but I caught the outline of the President and First Lady. I'd never had a feeling like it – pure adrenaline and elation; I felt as though I could pass out from the euphoria. "Thank you for making me do this," I whispered to Mad, who turned to me and clapped again, causing the audience to rise in ovation once more. It felt so remarkably real, even playing the piano. I felt every part of it, every key, every vibration. What Madeleine had created was truly the pinnacle of her life's work.

We walked backstage, my heart still thumping through my chest. "That was special," said Mad with a wobbly voice. It was the closest I think she'd ever come to crying. A deep man's voice startled me from behind the curtain.

"That was the most impressive thing I have ever seen." It was New Guy.

"What are you doing here?" I turned to look at Madeleine as she hurried off backstage, returning with two glasses of champagne, which she placed in our hands.

"Your friend called and said that I couldn't miss this, and she was right. I received the frisking of a lifetime from the bald guy at the Crypt entrance. He looked like he could have been in the Secret Service."

"Well, he actually was Secret Service. Check this out." I moved back the curtain slightly to show him the President of the United States. He looked genuinely flabbergasted. He'd only watched from behind the curtain and hadn't realised who we were playing for.

"Is that the Queen?" he asked, a little too loudly, not realising it was the end of the intermission, and the next performance was about to begin.

"Shhh," snapped Gergiev, as he left for the front of the stage for the next performance.

We stood back and watched as Benjamin Grosvenor took the stage. We watched from the side; New Guy stood so close behind me that I could feel his breath on the nape of my neck. I felt nervous energy the whole time. It felt remarkably real. After a few minutes, I looked around, but Mad and the orchestra had all left. It was just me and New Guy. Halfway through the performance, I leaned back and whispered, "Shall we go and get some drinks?" He nodded, and we started navigating our way towards the exit. I'd like to point out at this stage that if this weren't a simulation, I obviously would have waited around to meet the Obamas.

"Do you drink wine?" I asked as we stepped out onto the High Street.

"Does the Pope shit in the woods?" he responded.

"I know a place near here. It's the oldest wine bar in London." We started walking, and even though I knew this wasn't real, I felt nervous. How ridiculous was I! I couldn't even find confidence in my dreams! Luckily, New Guy broke the ice.

"I cannot even articulate how incredible that was to watch. I've seen you playing on YouTube, but it's even more extraordinary in person."

"You've watched me play online?"

"Of course. I love classical music. When I heard you'd played at The Royal Albert Hall, I had to see for myself."

"Oh yes, when the lovely Evelyn announced it to the room."

"Yeah, I wanted to talk to you about that! I'm not sure where you got the impression that we were dating, but it's not true. The only time we spent together was purely for work commitments."

"It's none of my business. I just assumed after you spent time together at her apartment and when I saw you on holiday at Christmas."

"Not at all. She heard I was going to the New York office and their Christmas party to see old colleagues and insisted I expense the flights to her father. I didn't realise she'd be going too, and she booked the seat next to me. To be honest, the whole thing was quite harrowing."

"And the things you left at her apartment?" As soon as I said it, I realised I sounded like a jealous girlfriend, trying to catch their partner out in a lie.

"She had a housewarming party, which was hideous. I misplaced my glasses, which I don't even remember taking. I stayed for an hour to be polite because hardly anyone showed up."

We'd reached the bar as he said this, and we perched on a pair of stools next to a table made from an old barrel. I took the liberty of ordering a bottle of Chateau Musar – it was Mad's red wine of choice. I kept going back to the Evelyn situation, as though running through the scenarios helped me persuade myself that maybe there was nothing going on between them.

"So, when you used to arrive at work together?"

"She'd be waiting for me in the foyer. The way I used to wait for you."

I looked up at him in surprise; it caught me off guard.

"You don't think it was a coincidence that I always happened to be downstairs whenever you arrived? Our elevator interactions were the highlight of my day."

Now that he mentioned it, it was him that was always waiting there – either in his car, on the phone outside, or in the foyer.

"And I have to say, when you came to us with the Evelyngate documents, it made so much sense! I assumed that Dick Fondler helped her. I had no idea how much plagiarism was going on. But of course, it was you writing everything. I am so sorry that you had to go through that."

"You have no idea. She was hell-bent on making my life miserable."

"She was jealous of you. You're talented, smart, and beautiful. She has a rich father who never gave her any attention and a plastic surgeon who clearly knows how to exploit the insecure."

"Ouch," I said, trying not to fall in love. "I still can't believe that she's gone. It seemed far too simple. But I can genuinely say that I hope she never comes back. In fact, can we make a pact to never speak of her again? She's consumed enough of my time as it is."

He raised his glass, and we clinked. We had a 'getting to know you' style date; the whole time I found myself transfixed by him. With Gomez, it was his humour that attracted me, and John was pure physical allure. New Guy had everything. He was intelligent, successful, funny, insanely handsome, and compassionate.

His mother was from Essex and his father from Croydon. They'd moved to the States for work, but both returned to the UK, which was why New Guy came home. He didn't want to be absent while his parents grew older. He was just fantastic. The conversation shifted towards Madeleine.

"We're going to need another bottle of that wine; you can't just describe Madeleine Magdalene in a few sips."

The bizarre thing about this evening was that I was starting to feel drunk. I suppose my brain was so used to my reactions to wine that I could recreate the physiological effects from muscle memory. I told him about the apartment I was living in and how the view was incredible. What was I trying to do, talk him into asking for an invite? This was my problem! I decided to take control.

"In fact, do you want to come back and have some wine on the rooftop?" His yes was instant. We quarrelled over who would settle the bill before he pretended to put me in a headlock so that the waiter would take his card. He whistled for a taxi, and although it didn't work, it was impressive. He tried to teach me how to whistle with my fingers, but I ended up spitting on my hand. We chatted and laughed the whole way back to the penthouse. When I turned the key, I heard the tinkling of little claws. Bingo! Of course I wanted him to be here in my simulation.

New Guy immediately dropped to the floor, just like Madeleine had at the dog rescue, and Bingo started squealing with happiness. He absolutely adored him. His expensive suit was now covered in fur and excitement pee. It filled my heart with joy that our little dog liked him. He had a good judge of character. New Guy wandered around the apartment in awe, just as I had when I woke up. I passed him a glass of champagne as he clocked the chess set.

"Fancy a game?" Could he be any more perfect?

"Sure! But come and see the view. We can take the board with us."

We stood atop the garden, calling out the buildings we could see. It was spectacular. He beat me twice before deciding to inform me that his grandfather was a grandmaster, so he played every Sunday growing up. We went back downstairs when it got chilly, and as I poured us some more wine, he picked up a guitar and began playing Romántica. He was good! He asked me to play piano again.

"Another time," I said.

"So, there will be another time?" he said, raising his eyebrow.

I realised that this would probably be the point where in real life we would kiss. It was one of those perfect moments. But I didn't want our first kiss to be in a simulation.

I motioned for us to sit on the sofa, and then he spotted my book. I was sure I put it in the bedroom.

"You've written a book?!" After reading the title, he informed me that he studied journalism with a philosophy major. I did already know this, having done my own research.

"May I read it?" he asked.

"Yeah, sure," I said, not realising he meant immediately. He sat back and started reading. It must have been because the day was so eventful, or because I wasn't used to my brain working in the simulation yet, but the next thing I knew, I woke up on my bed in the morning with Bingo on my toes. I turned to see if New Guy was next to me, but he wasn't. Bingo jumped up when I stirred and ran into the other room, wagging his tail. I could smell coffee. New Guy appeared at the door.

"I hope you don't mind that I stayed. I couldn't put down your book, and when I finished, I found another one. The society rats. They are both a triumph. I loved the illustrations of 'Ratbucks' and 'Rat A Manger.' Whenever Madeleine praised me, I never really took her opinion to heart, as she was so biased. I always sought an impartial outsider.

"I feel a bit embarrassed. I'm sorry I passed out like that; it was a lot to process in one day. But I'm so pleased you liked them."

"LOVED them," he corrected me. "How do you take your coffee? I have to head home and get changed before work, but I didn't want to be a bad houseguest. Mind if I take this little guy out to the park first? I think he needs to do his ablutions."

"Wow, yes, thank you. Milk, no sugar. The keys are on the sideboard by the entrance."

As he walked away, I chuckled to myself that perhaps my subconscious was being a little too idealistic. I couldn't imagine any man living up to these standards. I had only seen him at work, where, although he was a gentleman, he was there in a professional capacity. Most of the people from work weren't who they seemed to be outside the office. Take IT Adam. After five pints or more, he went from being kind and cheeky to impudent and contrarian. After pint seven, he verged on verbally abusive. When New Guy came back with Bingo, he brought some pastries. I stood at the bedroom doorway in my silk gown as he thanked me for an extraordinary evening.

"I'll see you in an hour," I said with a smile. He looked a little perplexed, perhaps because I didn't come to the door to see him out. Damn, that was rude of me. Simulation me had lost all manners.

21

Work felt incredible without Evelyn there. I finally had the position I'd worked so hard for. It felt entirely rejuvenating. I popped to the kitchen, tapping my cup as I walked past New Guy's office, to which he gave me a thumbs up. I knew how he took his coffee; I'd watched him rummage around most mornings looking for sugar and a spoon. As I placed it on his desk, I casually said, "I've been asked to review a new French bistro in Shoreditch. Fancy some dinner this week?" Without hesitation, he leaned back in his chair and said, "How about tonight?" Was it that easy? Was that all I had to do?

Another fantastic dinner. We drank great wine and ate mediocre food. I had hoped that my first official review would be more positive, but sadly, it was 'fur coat, no knickers.' My company, however, was five stars – would recommend. I once more decided to avoid anything intimate. It would be like kissing an imaginary friend. It felt cheap, desperate even. Even though I could imagine what a hazelnut dacquoise tasted like in remarkable detail, I'd tried that before. How could I possibly imagine what a night with a man like New Guy would feel like?

I was only four days into the experience, but I felt fully immersed. I had done everything I'd want to do, and I felt like I wanted to be back as myself as quickly as possible, so I could implement everything I'd conceived. Apart from the ridiculously expensive apartment – I didn't have that kind of money. I took Bingo downstairs after work and hopped in the town car. I wanted to go and see my friend. We arrived back at the house, and Bingo urinated in the kitchen from excitement when he was reunited with his mum.

"Back so soon!" yelped Madeleine. "What's happened? Who's upset you now?"

"Welcome home to you too! Nothing's happened. No one has upset me! In fact, I think this has been the best week of my life. I just wanted to see you, so you were a part of it! I can't wait to be back with the real Madeleine to tell her how incredible this environment is. Everything is so real, so beautiful, so convincing."

Madeleine started smirking. "Libel, squeeze those limes. We're going to make a jug of margaritas and have a little chat."

Mad placed an obscene amount of tequila into a jug of crushed ice and salted the rims of some glasses. "Follow me," she beckoned, wagging her index finger towards the lab. Delilah looked surprised to see me. Her hair was tied back in a messy ponytail, and her skin was its usual shade of grey.

"Delilah," began Mad, "what general anaesthetic have we used on the test subjects for the experiment thus far?"

Delilah looked confused, and Mad nodded. "It's not a trick, I'm just educating young Elizabeth."

"Propofol."

"And what drug did we use on Elizabeth on Sunday?"

"Phenobarbital."

"What's the difference?"

"Propofol is used for deep sedation; it makes the subject completely unconscious until the anaesthetist stops the anaesthetic. Phenobarbital is a sedative that sends you into a deep sleep, but it wears off naturally over time."

"Why did we only give Elizabeth a sedative?"

"Because you didn't put Elizabeth into the simulation."

Mad turned back towards me. "Because we didn't put you into the simulation. Everything you've done this week has been entirely you."

I laughed as I took a sip of my tequila. "Is that so? So, explain a few things for me, if you wouldn't mind. The penthouse apartment?"

"That's my uncle's apartment. He uses it if he ever comes to London. I just added a few things to make it more 'you.'"

"So, if I go upstairs to my room?"

"It will be all the crap I didn't think necessary to clutter up the apartment with. Which was most of it."

"OK, Rats for Dinner, how did you finish that in time?"

"Lizzy, I had it finished, bound, and printed in an afternoon. It was partly why I was so frustrated with you. I could have done it the whole time, but I didn't want to have to."

"And my other book?"

"Yeah, that was a bit harder. Your notes and first draft were scrambled eggs. It was also brilliant and only needed a touch of love to amalgamate it all. That took me most of the week. Victoria, my personal shopper, sorted out your wardrobe (you look fantastic, by the way), and Dan Chan organised the delivery of the instruments. What do you think of that Bösendorfer?"

"Um, yeah, it's magnificent."

"So, we sedated you, tossed you in the back of the Range Rover, and drove you down to Portman Square. We were worried at one point when we misjudged a speed bump that you'd wake up. You were so high; you didn't even twitch."

This was the point where I began to suspect that Madeleine was being serious. Then I asked the question that would plague me for the foreseeable future.

"How do I know that I'm not still in the simulation, imagining this whole conversation? What if I'm creating this scenario to convince myself that the world I imagined is real?"

"As we've discussed before, I don't think you have it in you. You're too indecisive for a start! Also, I have a question. Did you know what phenobarbital or propofol was before today? Because if not, I'm fairly sure you wouldn't be able to conjure scientific knowledge."

"No. I guess I didn't."

"You have the internet, go and Google things you don't know the answer to."

"So, you're telling me that I exposed Evelyn to my boss, played piano in front of the Queen, snubbed Barack Obama, invited New Guy back to the apartment twice, and didn't touch him – and that was all real?"

"Wait, you had that hot man back to your apartment and nothing happened?"

"I didn't want the first time anything happened between us to be in my imagination. I thought it was all make-believe, remember?"

"Wow. Having seen him up close and in person, you must be the first straight woman ever to turn him down."

"I didn't turn him down."

"He went for drinks with you, came back to your flat, told you he waited for you every morning at work, and that you were beautiful. I'm fairly sure that was him showing interest."

"Oh."

"Oh, indeed."

"I feel a bit nauseated, knowing that it actually happened. It was fine when I thought it was all theoretical. Oh my God, Mad, what if I'd punched Evelyn in the face?"

"When have you ever punched anyone in the face?"

"I've thought about it."

"You've thought about many things and never done them. That's your problem."

"So, what now? I can't keep living in that gorgeous apartment; I couldn't afford the rent."

"It's yours for as long as you want it. My uncle hasn't been home for years, it's just sat there accruing value and dust. He was pleased someone was enjoying it. But you have to come and stay here every other weekend. You can't just get a boyfriend and disappear into the abyss."

"I don't know what to say."

"I do. Message your American boy, go back to the city, and take his clothes off for crying out loud. If you don't, someone else will!"

"This is all so much to process. What if it all goes horribly wrong?"

"That was, of course, a risk. You could have lost your job, been rejected by New Guy, and been dreadfully offended that I finished your life's work. But it didn't, so yay!"

"I am equally annoyed and grateful that you manipulated my life like that."

"You're welcome. I knew you had it in you! You were your own worst enemy. And I love you too."

I decided to stay at Gethsemane House that night, but I didn't sleep well. I kept firing questions at Mad, and she was right: she was telling me things I had no prior knowledge of, things I couldn't have just imagined. They could also not have been the correct answers. I couldn't corroborate the validity of what she said. It could all have been complete nonsense. When Madeleine mentioned that the atomic number for polonium was eighty-four, how could I know I hadn't just made that up? It was exhausting, constantly second-guessing myself.

I'd spent years struggling with so many issues and situations; it seemed unlikely that I could simply turn my life around in a few days. I scrutinised the room to see if anything in the flat was duplicated, but it didn't appear so. I kept thinking of my dad telling me that if something seemed too good to be true, it probably wasn't. I worried I could drive myself mad with doubt.

The next morning, I set off for work. It was a beautiful, sunny day, without a cloud in the sky. Petra waited at her gate for me, which was odd. She then lifted a small, ten-week-old puppy up for me to see. "He's called Randy, in tribute to his brother."

I couldn't let Madeleine know about this. It takes a resilient man to hand a puppy back to its owner—a strength Madeleine lacked. I played with the puppy far longer than I should have and had to adopt a brisk pace when I finally left. Then I heard a little 'toot toot' from Rory's Mini as he slowed to a stop and wound down his window to offer me a lift. We got to Archway before I decided to get the tube from there; the traffic was far too slow. I arrived at work with a coffee and a pastry, somehow managing to be on time. We filed into the morning meeting, with Daphne standing at the head of the table to make an announcement.

"As I'm sure you all know, we recently discovered plagiarism under our own roof. Although the person responsible is no longer with us, there remained the issue of the BJ Awards nomination. We don't believe it's fair for hard work to go unacknowledged, so the committee has agreed that the credit will still stand—but be given to its rightful recipient. Can we all give a round of applause to Elizabeth Angelo?"

Everyone clapped, and it was just as embarrassing as the last time they did it.

"We'll be having champagne in the meeting room this Friday, should anyone wish to join us in wishing her the best of luck."

Again, it was all a little too convenient. As everyone filed out, I stayed seated. I was sceptical. Everything was going a bit too well. I was paranoid that I was still caught in the experiment; despite everything Mad said, I felt uneasy. It wasn't that I didn't trust Madeleine—if I were still in the experiment, it would be my subconscious I couldn't trust. I'd suffered from imposter syndrome for as long as I could remember, something I hadn't mentioned to Madeleine during the psychometric testing. I'd been doubting myself for such a long time, so it stood to reason that I'd doubt this too. New Guy held back, asking if everything was okay. I sat, pondering what my next move should be.

I came out with it straight away, asking him to be my plus-one for the awards. No fumbling, no worrying it would be too awkward. I was concise and assertive.

"Absolutely," he said, without hesitation. I nodded, he nodded, and I walked back to my desk. Throughout the afternoon, I struggled to concentrate. I found myself reading the same paragraph two or three times without actually taking it in. This went on all afternoon. I was worrying about so many things and questioning my very existence. I felt paranoid that most of the songs on the office radio were about dreaming or waking up. I wasn't a fan of coincidences at the best of times. I stayed at Madeleine's that night but couldn't sleep.

My scepticism was only heightened by an early morning encounter with Veruschka, who unleashed a barrage of abuse. A crazed gypsy screaming, "You need to open your eyes" when you're already worried you might be trapped in a VR simulation wasn't exactly helpful. She must have sensed my hesitation. I don't even know why I stopped.

"Why do you keep telling Madeleine and me to open our eyes?" I asked, unexpectedly aggressive.

"You know why," she repeated for the thousandth time.

"I don't know why! I don't understand why you taunt us."

"I am only here because you want me to be. I am the truth." As she said this, she moved the shrubbery covering the house sign, which read 'Veritas.'

"Why must you speak in riddles? You stand here saying terrifying things, phoning our house and being cryptic, all the while your daughter is locked in the attic."

"My daughter? No, dear, I don't have a daughter. If you looked a little closer, you'd see the truth. The girl who is trapped is you."

I was glad she said that. Compared to her, I felt far less crazy. I walked to the station, feeling slightly less concerned about the ramblings of a lunatic. The problem was that, because I was consciously looking for signs that I was trapped, I kept finding them. It was like when I found out about Gomez, and suddenly all I heard were love songs, and all I saw were people in love. Of course, those things are always around, but it's only because you're seeking them that you notice them.

I passed a billboard that read 'Wake Up'—an advert for coffee. Then I heard 'Wake Up, Little Susie' from a car radio. I put my headphones in, and the first song on shuffle was 'Exit Music' by Radiohead, the haunting words 'wake from your sleep' enough to make me take them out again. I had been overthinking everything. I couldn't shake the feeling that something wasn't right. I felt almost manic with paranoia. I began squeezing my fists and digging my nails into my palms, trying to feel present—something I used to do when I had panic attacks before going on stage. I felt like I was completely Mad.

New Guy poured out of his car with smooth elegance, acknowledging my arrival with a beaming smile. As we walked towards the lift, he was talking, but I wasn't listening. I was in a trance-like state. As the doors closed on the empty lift, I snapped out of it and decided to kiss him, just to see if it felt authentic. It was a nice kiss. Nice didn't exactly rattle my bones. I'd thought about this moment for months, and though it was reciprocated, it wasn't the crescendo I'd imagined. Was it because I wasn't mindfully present, or because I wasn't present at all? It didn't quash my concerns about being cataleptic in a lab. Nothing else was said as I stepped out and walked towards my desk. I did turn back to see him still smiling at me, which, I admit, made me a little giddy.

I felt trapped in a nightmare. Just like Veruschka said. I wasn't happy before because I was stuck in my own fear, and now I was unhappy because I feared I was stuck.. And then the question that scared me the most: if I obtained irrefutable proof that I was still in the simulation, how could I wake up?

At that moment of excruciating doubt, Michael Jackson sent me an email. Good timing. I asked him to meet me at The World's End. It was 11:08 a.m., but he was already there, as if it were the headquarters for his operation. He was cradling a pint, his hair glued in place, and a pack of cigarettes already half gone. I asked him how much it would cost to investigate Madeleine's parents, her uncle, Veruschka, and Veruschka's daughter. He was impossibly vague, suggesting it could take weeks or months, meaning either hundreds or thousands. Then he said, "We could always come to another arrangement," his eyes wandering towards my feet.

"You want my Jimmy Choos?"

"I want some photos of your feet."

"Ew, yuk. Every time I meet you, you manage to add another page of creepiness to your CV."

"My time is precious, and so are the delicate curves of a feminine foot."

"I feel unclean just talking to you about it. Find out what you can. Cash, as always, will be the commodity of choice."

I didn't know how this would help me. It felt as though knowledge was key, albeit contradictory if this was my own mind providing said knowledge. I suppose I wanted to hear things I didn't think I knew. I was unravelling. Madeleine was growing increasingly annoyed at both me and herself for allowing this to happen.

"I wish you'd told me beforehand that you were this fucking delusional," she hissed, moving her queen to E4. "You never showed me this hysterical side of you. I'd have beaten it out of you years ago if I'd known."

"Madeleine, I specialised in philosophy. Of course, I question everything."

The evening of the awards ceremony arrived, and I should have felt excited, but I was numb. I sat staring into the gaze of the stranger in the mirror. I wore a long silk gown, shoes I could never have afforded, and a handbag that cost more than a month's salary. The intercom sounded, so I finished my glass of champagne and skipped over to buzz New Guy up. Except it wasn't him. It was the doorman. "I have Michael Jackson downstairs. Shall I send him up?" I wondered how he knew where I lived, but I concluded it wasn't outside the remit of a private investigator. "I'll come down, thank you." I certainly didn't want him in my flat, sniffing my socks or perving over my shoe closet.

He handed me the envelope, with a rather perplexed expression. "This Veruschka and her daughter—it's like they don't exist. Stranger still, her house doesn't show on any of the original site plans for the estate. It's like both she and the building just appeared."

"Michael, you're not making any sense."

"Well, if you don't like that, you won't like the next part. David and Elizabeth—it's like they both just, well, disappeared. They have dual passports, but they haven't used either of them. There's no activity in the bank accounts, save for direct debits. I can't see any use of their email or phones, and there are no hospital or police records. They've just vanished off the grid."

"And the uncle?"

"Yeah, he checks out—as much as I can get on him. He's richer than God. Getting anywhere near him has been impossible. You'd be better off just googling him."

"I don't feel like you've provided any answers, Michael. You've just raised more questions."

"Yeah, I felt that way too. Look, no charge. I don't really want to get involved with this."

Michael Jackson looked perturbed. He hadn't liked what he'd uncovered, and neither did I. When New Guy arrived in the limousine, I should have been elated. But I felt hopeless. I couldn't enjoy the moment. If this was real, I was ruining the best night of my life. We shared a kiss in the back seat, but I felt nothing. All I could do was worry about the bizarre findings from Michael Jackson.

When they announced me as the winner of the BJ Awards, I all but shrugged as I stood and trudged to the stage. Later, while everyone enjoyed drinks and different people approached me to commend and congratulate me, I wasn't even listening. New Guy looked incredibly handsome in his tuxedo; looking at him made all my doubts dissolve. He was so kind, smart, and perfect. Too perfect. Everything about the last few weeks was just too perfect.

I stood at the bar, waiting for another champagne. New Guy crept up next to me, placing his hand on the small of my back, "There you are," I found it hard to look at him without smiling. Even the small touch made me tremble. Then, as if following a script, he went and spoiled it all by saying something stupid. "I think I'm falling in love with you." As soon as he said it, I was crushed with sadness. People don't fall in love that quickly. Life wasn't that fair. I smiled at him, and stroked his shoulder. "I'll be right back."

I ghosted the party and jumped into a cab to Madeleine's. As we approached the house, I saw Veruschka standing by her rusty gate and asked the driver to pull over. I shouldn't have stopped.

"I spoke to an investigator about you. He seems to think that you and all this don't exist. What's your explanation, Veruschka? Are you even who you say you are? Are you withholding that girl's freedom in your loft?"

Veruschka put down the basket of apples she was holding and slithered up to the gate. I immediately stepped back.

"I am the voice in your head that you cannot ignore. I am the feeling you have when something isn't right. It is you that is trapped inside the attic, Madeleine. Open your eyes." I looked up to see the silhouette of the young girl, her pale skin and long blonde hair. She looked strikingly like Mad.

She had poisoned my thoughts.

"Why did you call me Madeleine? I am not Madeleine."

"Open your eyes. You are one and the same," she said, as she walked towards her house. I called out after her, but she continued inside. Enough was enough. Her cryptic comments and taunts were driving me mad. I pushed through the corroded gate and walked towards the rotten stoop. Goosebumps formed as I shuddered from the uncertainty. I could sense the house daring me to stay away. I reached the threshold and felt as though I physically couldn't go any further.

The door had been left ajar, and I tentatively pushed it open with my fingertips. I wasn't sure what I was expecting to see, but I wasn't expecting a beautiful family home. Completely at odds with the hellish exterior, it was warm and inviting, with peaches and yellows, trinkets, and paintings. There were plants and flowers, and the smell of freshly baked bread. It made it even more frightening somehow. As I looked around, out of nowhere, a blurry figure—one with the likeness of Madeleine—ran from behind the stairs and slammed the door shut. It made me jump, and I almost choked from gasping. Whatever it was, it didn't want me there. I knocked for a while, calling out Veruschka's name, but she didn't answer.

I felt terrified and confused. I hurried back to Madeleine's, in through the soulless entrance, and down the hallway, passing the panelled walls with the faded paint where portraits used to hang. She was sitting in the living room, curled up on the sofa with Bingo, watching Mastermind. "We need to talk," I said, in the sternest voice I'd ever used with her. She switched off the TV and turned to me, saying, "You have my attention."

"I asked Michael Jackson to look into Veruschka, and it's like she doesn't exist. I stopped on my way and saw her, and she said it was you in the window, and then she called me Madeleine? What did she mean by it? Why did she say you were the one trapped? Why did she call me Madeleine?"

"Elizabeth, you need to calm down. She's an absolute maniac. Listen to me, you need to ignore her. She's a crazy old kook, and everyone thinks so. I am not in Veruschka's loft."

"I can't handle this." It felt as though someone was crushing my brain. I couldn't understand what was happening to me.

"Elizabeth, you are not stuck in a simulation. You are trying to self-sabotage as everything you've ever wanted is starting to manifest, and for some reason, you don't think you deserve it. I don't know why you trust a man who calls himself Michael Jackson, who works from a Camden boozer and masturbates over people's toenails."

I knew I had to show her what Michael Jackson had given me. I stood up to go and fetch the file and some wine. It was finally time that I knew everything.

"It's not just him, Madeleine. I saw you, at least a version of you at Veruschka's house. I'm losing my mind trying to figure out what's real."

Madeleine reached out and clutched my hand.

"Elizabeth, relax. You're just as real as I am."

23

December 19th, 2008

It was the second time that DCI John Polglase had attended Magdalene Mansion, this time with Detective Twyning, a force support group, and a warrant. The first time was to investigate a report of a potential aggravated assault, which turned out to be next door. None of the houses on the road were numbered, and they'd accidentally wandered up to Gethsemane House. A woman in her twenties, presumably Madeleine, had opened the door to him. There was some sort of party underway, and she had tried relentlessly to get John to join in. He apologised and went on his way, not before having to fend her off as she tugged at his arm. Why was he blushing, he thought. She was incredibly inappropriate, and this was hugely unprofessional. The young lady had stuck in his mind, and so when he found himself back here, he'd hoped it was a mistake.

At the same time, officers presented themselves at the property next door. Thomas Carrigan, who had called in the matter, stood sheepishly as they informed him that officers were forcibly entering his neighbour's house. "How long have you known the Magdalene's?" the detective asked as she flipped open her notebook, nodding in gratitude as Rory placed down cups of tea for her and her colleague.

"We've only been to their house once in the time they've lived here, for their Christmas party. Almost everybody on the street attended."

"Had Mr Magdalene been in contact with you prior to last night?"

"No, never. The only person we ever really saw was their daughter when we passed her on the way to work in the morning. We'd only met her once, at the party, but she was nice."

Rory interrupted, "Oh my god, she was so nice. She and her mother were adorable."

"You told my colleague on the phone that Mr Magdalene approached you yesterday evening seeking your advice in a medical capacity?"

"Yes. He said his wife and daughter both suffered from amyotrophic lateral sclerosis, and he needed some advice from a neurologist. He was almost incoherent, practically dragging me across the road."

"Can you describe what you saw when you arrived at the house?"

"I didn't go into the house. It was a laboratory accessed through the side of the property. It was like walking onto the Starship Enterprise."

The officers shuddered as they walked down the freezing, dark corridors; the furniture smelled musty and was covered in thick dust.

The only room they couldn't enter was accessible via a keypad entry system. A solid metal, seemingly impenetrable vault. They knocked twice, then three times, with no answer. John announced himself. "David, it's Detective Chief Inspector Polglase. I need you to open the door. Failure to do so will result in forced entry." Nothing. They waited a minute and knocked again, issuing a final warning. John stood back, allowing the technical team to bypass the entry code. As the pad turned green, John cautiously pushed the door open, revealing David Magdalene. He was thin, emaciated, with pure white hair that seemed premature for his age. He sat slumped over an unconscious woman, holding her hand. She was connected to monitors and breathing machines. The name in the top right corner of the screen read, 'Elizabeth Magdalene.'

David peered up at the detective, his bloodshot eyes watering from exhaustion and despair. "They won't wake up," he quivered, his grey, dehydrated lips trembling. There was another bed, with another woman, also unconscious and wired to equipment and drips.

As John had feared, it was Madeleine.

David and Jude

When David and Jude first pitched the neurochip to Madeleine's uncle, he and his team were overwhelmed with enthusiasm. It was unheard-of technology, incredibly innovative. They invested in the project immediately, and when the first VR headset was produced, they were absolutely blown away. Jude, a neuroscientist, had plans to take it further—to engineer a chip that could be implanted in the brain to control the user's thoughts and provide a real-life experience. Everyone, apart from David, was nervous. The impact this could have on people who'd suffered brain injuries! The possibilities were limitless. This wasn't a recreational invention; it was going to change how we accessed parts of the human mind.

Three years passed. David continued to help his brother-in-law with various projects, his daughter Madeleine becoming involved while she began her studies at Oxford. Nothing could have made him prouder. His insanely talented daughter was a chip off the old block. Thankfully, she had her mother's beauty and generosity. After a day doing what he loved, he'd walk back to his magnificent home to find the two most important people in his life laughing together on the balcony. He understood almost everything there was to know about physics, computers, and biology, but he could never comprehend how he had become so lucky.

By late 2007, David and Jude flew to Palo Alto to meet with the board and discuss the project's progress. Medical specialists and neurologists flew in from around the world, and the scientists eagerly awaited the next stage of funding to apply for human trials. The day was full of questions, data analysis, risk assessments, testing the clinical development, and the effects on animal models. Jude batted away any queries or doubts—this couldn't fail. There was a unanimous vote that there wasn't enough evidence to support the project being safe enough for human trials. The experts all agreed that the risk was too high and there were too many possible psychological anomalies. They concluded that there wasn't enough information available about the effects of VR on the hippocampus. Their main concern was the subject's inability to delineate between the real and the unreal. There was also concern that the hippocampus could be damaged during implantation.

They were halting funding until there was a greater understanding of the effects of augmented exposure. "A few more years of preliminary research," David comforted. "That's all that's needed."

Jude was furious. He was adamant they were all wrong. David was saddened. If they didn't think they were there yet, they could be. It felt dismissive to simply halt their progress. Jude became more and more obsessed with continuing their work. He tried to persuade David to seek financial help from his wife. She spoke with her brother, who refused to contribute to the project his experts had just vetoed. Determined that he was being gaslighted, Jude remortgaged his own house, applying for UK trials to take place. He took out loans and sought investors, becoming increasingly desperate to finish his life's work. He had studied this subject for his entire career, and he knew they were on the brink of something groundbreaking. They could improve millions of lives and help better understand a myriad of diseases.

But by early 2008, everything was put on hold. For David, at least. His beloved wife, Elizabeth, had suddenly become ill. At first, it was silly things. She became forgetful, which, for someone with an eidetic memory, was concerning. Her concentration was limited, and she'd become agitated easily, despite being passive and patient her entire life. The anger was compounded by the fact that she had suddenly become clumsy, constantly dropping things, or bumping into furniture. Then, one evening at dinner, Madeleine noticed her mother slurring her words. The next day, David called on Jude to take blood and urine samples for tests.

He sat David down first, telling him his wife had early-stage amyotrophic lateral sclerosis. David couldn't speak. He kept insisting Jude was wrong, until he showed him the results. David had seen her symptoms for himself. She had less than a year to live and would decline rapidly.

They sat down together to tell her, explaining the next stages and that there wasn't a cure. While the couple sobbed in each other's arms, Jude focused on the matter at hand. He told them they needed to assess Madeleine. It was possible it could be passed on to her genetically. David fell apart at the thought of losing them both.

David immediately dismissed the suggestion of his wife partaking in the simulation. The idea that she would be suspended in time, her body and mind decaying more slowly, merely delaying the inevitable. But she volunteered. For her, at the very least, her legacy could help with their study. At best, it could help regenerate nerve cells and provide insights that could save Madeleine. There was nothing she wouldn't do to protect her daughter. She'd try it for a day first. Elizabeth begged David not to tell Madeleine what she was doing, but he knew he couldn't keep anything from his daughter, especially if something happened to her mother.

Madeleine, being of a scientific mind, could see the potential benefits and understood her mother's willingness to take part. The less practical part of her was horrified they would risk anything happening to someone so important. When she tried to argue with her father, he explained it was out of his control. She was dying. They had to do something. Madeleine was horrified—what an impossible situation to be in. When she confided in her father, seeking alternative solutions, he dismissed her, believing she was letting emotions get in the way of scientific fact. There was no cure. The only way to help her mother was to try something radical. He knew available research had exhausted all avenues for a cure.

Jude took samples from Madeleine. He told David that she too had the ALS mutation. David hid from his daughter and wept. He had never known such agonising pain. Nothing mattered except them. How would he survive without their love?

Two hours had passed since the anaesthetic wore off, yet Elizabeth remained asleep. They monitored every detail of her condition, and everything seemed positive. After four hours, they began running tests. After six hours, Madeleine started to lose control, screaming at her father, demanding to know why her mother hadn't woken up. She hadn't realised her mother was patient zero. What kind of monster would use the love of their life as a lab rat? David didn't have the heart to tell her the news that this too was her fate.

Jude couldn't understand what had happened. Perhaps the benzodiazepine he used to induce ALS symptoms had interfered with the process. It would be fine once the drug worked its way out of her system, he thought. This had nothing to do with his chip. He was livid he hadn't waited for the drug to wear off before inducing her. After everything he'd risked—his marriage, his house, his life savings, his reputation—he couldn't be wrong. This technology was transformative. He was going to change the direction of psychological experiments; he would go down in history for his contributions to science.

After two days without sleep, Jude and David worked tirelessly to find a way to wake her. They continued to play subliminal cues and songs to remind them they were still in the experiment. David wanted nothing more than to speak to his wife, to see her smile, to know she was okay. Jude was desperate to learn about her experience. She was the key to everything he'd worked for. She would tell him how it felt, how realistic the world was, whether smell and taste translated from memory to the experiment. How did time there correlate to time experienced in waking hours? They had concluded that a day in real life would equate to about a month in the simulation. Finally, they would have definitive answers. Another day passed. Then another. They were growing delirious. When David suggested it might be time to get his wife some help, Jude rose to his feet and shouted, "Our emotional priorities must yield to the future of science as we know it."

24

December 19th, 2008

Polglase shrugged when his colleague asked what they would do when the ambulances arrived. "Go and fetch the neurologist who called this in. To be honest, Sarge, I haven't got the faintest idea how to handle this." When David Magdalene overheard the word "ambulance," he began to unravel. "You can't take them! You can't disconnect them! They're on life support!"

Officers moved closer, ready to restrain him if necessary, but David lacked the strength to put up any resistance. He shielded his daughter with his frail frame, and even as he lay over her, his heavy eyes were beginning to close. Polglase knew the man needed help before he could be questioned.

Thomas arrived around the same time as the ambulance, rounding the corner awkwardly, worried that David might know it was him who had alerted the authorities. Thomas knelt down beside David and, in a calm, clear voice, began, "David, we need to take the girls to the hospital so they can have CT scans. We need to find out why they're still in a coma. You also need medical attention." Polglase added, "We could use your input, but not in the state you're in. You're sleep-deprived, dehydrated, and malnourished." David nodded, defeated. Eventually, the men agreed to take the women to the hospital. David would also receive treatment so that he could provide a statement under caution.

Minutes from Police Interview - Case Number 2008666

Officers Present - DCI John Polglase, Detective Elowen Twyning

Interviewee - David Magdalene

Date - December 20th, 2008

JP - Present for this interview are myself, Detective Chief Inspector John Polglase, Detective Elowen Twyning, and David Magdalene. David, you have been cautioned, but for the purposes of this interview, may I remind you that you do not have to say anything, but anything you do say may be used as evidence in court. You have the right to legal representation, which you have refused, though you can request counsel at any time. This interview is being recorded, and you may end it whenever you wish. Do you understand? Please respond with "yes" or "no" for the recording.

DM - Yes.

JP - David, in your own words, can you describe the events that have led to your wife and daughter being in a vegetative state?

DM - I was informed by a neurologist that my wife was suffering from ALS, an incurable neurodegenerative disease. She consented, under the Nuremberg Code, for us to trial an experimental treatment to delay or possibly reverse her condition.

JP - Did you or your wife consult any other physician besides (shuffling papers) Dr Jude Peters?

DM - We didn't. It wasn't until after Dr Peters fled that I conducted further tests myself and realised the previous data had been manipulated.

JP - And your daughter, Madeleine? Did she consent to the experiment under the Nuremberg Code?

(Long pause)

DM - Madeleine was only believed to carry the enzyme for the disease. She should never have been included in the experiment.

JP - You claim that Dr Peters involved your daughter in the testing without your knowledge, and that he denied you access to the laboratory while doing so?

DM - He changed the lab's door code, and it was only when he couldn't wake Madeleine either that he reopened the entrance and fled.

JP - And you didn't try to stop him?

DM - My priority was to get inside and check on my family. Confronting him wasn't my focus at that moment.

JP - Don't you find it rather convenient that Dr Peters' house is empty, and his wife says she hasn't seen him in months?

DM - I'd say it's the opposite of convenient, considering he's the one responsible for this.

JP - Yet you both developed this (shuffling papers) neuropathic chip together, and your wife's brother was financing the research?

DM - Yes, but it was in its infancy. Jude became infatuated, even obsessed, with the project. He was drugging my family and manipulating data to convince them they had brain damage.

JP - And at no point did you, a Harvard-educated scientist, find it suspicious that, shortly after your human trials were denied, a situation arose where the product you were working on became potentially useful?

DM - I had no reason to distrust Jude. He specialised in electromyography and nerve conduction studies; he was an expert. I never imagined he'd put Madeleine or Elizabeth in danger for the sake of research. It wasn't something I considered while facing the possibility of losing both my girls.

JP - So you're saying he knew you'd do anything to save your wife, even if it meant making hasty, irrational decisions?

DM - It wasn't hasty or irrational. ALS is a ticking time bomb. Her results indicated she could have a week, a month, or a year before irreversible decline.

JP - Results that didn't exist?

DM - They did exist, but they were forged. Her symptoms were very real.

JP - And what symptoms were those?

DM - The symptoms consistent with ALS.

JP - You claim that, upon conducting your own blood tests, you found evidence of benzodiazepines in your daughter's system, and that this was significant?

DM - The side effects of benzodiazepines overlap with many ALS symptoms: tremors, confusion, derealisation—all of which my wife experienced. It was evident she wasn't mentally present.

JP - Yet you accepted Dr Peters' diagnosis without considering the similarity between those side effects and benzodiazepines?

DM - Yes because she wasn't taking any medication. I can only assume Jude was administering the drugs without her knowledge.

JP - How would Dr Peters have had the opportunity to drug your wife for an extended period, Mr Magdalene?

DM - He'd been staying at our house for months. He'd released a large amount of equity from his family home without his wife's consent to fund the project, and they were arguing. He needed somewhere to stay. He always made breakfast. (Mr Magdalene begins crying) Oh God, I let that man poison my family.

(Detective Twyning hands the suspect a tissue)

DM - He always made freshly squeezed orange juice. The girls wouldn't have realised they were being drugged.

JP - But Madeleine didn't initially show any symptoms?

DM - Not at first. After her mother became ill, she tried to prevent the experiment. She was adamantly against it. I would never have allowed her to trial the chip; her brain was too young.

JP - But you didn't mind your wife's brain being tampered with?

DM - Please don't twist my words, Detective. I didn't think I had any other choice.

JP - Why did you conduct the experiment in your own home, when all previous research had taken place in high-tech labs in the United States?

DM - We conducted research in our lab too. The laboratory at my home mirrors almost all the equipment available at those facilities. We had some of the best and most advanced apparatus in the UK at our disposal.

JP - The problem, Mr Magdalene, is that we have no evidence of Dr Peters' involvement. We can't find him to question, and both victims are unconscious indefinitely. There's no evidence of consent, and all we have is the word of the man whose experiment went wrong. So why didn't they wake up after the chips were removed?

DM - That's what neither of us can understand.

JP - "Us"?

DM - Dr Peters and I, before he absconded. They should've woken up as soon as the chip was removed. It was meant to be temporary. The animals we experimented on recovered within minutes; there was no indication of long-term interference.

JP - Perhaps Dr Peters tampered with those results too?

DM - I was present throughout that stage of the process. We were advised by leading neurologists who were shocked we weren't granted approval.

JP - I'm not a brain surgeon, Dr Magdalene, but I know the human brain is far more complex than that of a rat. Especially if the subjects were as gifted as Mrs Magdalene and Madeleine. How did Dr Peters persuade Madeleine to participate?

DM - She never would have agreed. She probably doesn't even realise she's part of an experiment.

JP - Which leads me to my next question. How did she become a participant in the first place? You claim Dr Peters sedated her, but how did he manage that, and why didn't you try to stop him?

DM - (raised voice) Madeleine was already asleep in the lab after her mother was sedated. She wanted to be near her. I'd left the lab, and he wouldn't let me back in until it was too late.

JP - Why did you leave the lab?

DM - To have a shower, eat—I can't remember. We were in and out all the time.

JP - So Dr Peters didn't let you back in until he realised your daughter wouldn't wake up?

DM - That's what I said. She doesn't even know she's in a simulation.

JP - So you're saying your daughter is trapped in her own dream?

DM - I'm saying both she and her mother are. They'll only wake up when they realise they're asleep.

JP - And until then?

DM - We turn to God.

JP - Before we conclude, Dr Magdalene, could you provide a list of any close friends or acquaintances of Madeleine's—anyone we could speak to who's had recent contact with her?

DM - There's no one. She never really had friends. She had a boyfriend in Australia, but we never met him. To be honest, we thought she'd made him up.

JP - So there's no one else? University friends, colleagues, any clubs?

DM - If there are, my wife would know better. No one I can think of.

JP - Do you have any family we could speak to?

DM - Not in the UK. Her uncle is in the US, and her sister, Evelyn, lives in Australia, but they're not close.

JP - If you could provide their details, we'd like to follow up.

Interview suspended at 9:15 am.

"You'd better hope your wife and daughter wake up, Dr Magdalene. This doesn't look good for you."

"I want nothing else."

Dr Magdalene left the room, while Twyning and Polglase deliberated.

"What do you think, John?"

"I don't like it. Something feels off. I met Madeleine last year, and she didn't strike me as someone without friends. The fact we can't find Jude Peters, and he hasn't used his passport or bank card in four weeks. And there's just something about that man. I can't put my finger on it."

"He doesn't seem present."

"I think he's upset, but not because his family won't wake up."

"Because the experiment failed?"

Polglase stood from his desk and walked towards the window. "I'm not sure. But my gut says he's not to be trusted."

"What struck me as odd was a scientist saying he'd turn to God."

"Didn't you find it even stranger that their mansion is called Gethsemane?" Twyning shrugged, not understanding the reference. "It's the garden where Judas betrayed Jesus." Polglase sifted through some papers, refocusing on the house's contents.

"What did the search team recover from Madeleine's room?"

"The report says the room was bare. Hardly any belongings. You wouldn't think it was a 20 something-year-old's room."

"No diary?"

"John, it's 2008. People don't have diaries; they have Facebook." John's eyes lit up like a Christmas tree. Within minutes, they found Madeleine Magdalene, London. The account was private, and they forwarded it to IT to unlock. "We need a glimpse into this girl's life. Somebody must know something."

A knock sounded at the door, and an officer stepped in. "There's a girl in reception you might want to speak to." John walked down the stairs into the waiting room. A young woman in her early twenties, who looked remarkably like Winona Ryder (during the Johnny Depp years), was pacing impatiently.

"How can I help you, Ms Angelo?"

Elizabeth rushed to the Inspector, fear swimming in her eyes.

"I think something's happened to my best friend."